Law Firm Mergers

Lessons from Successful Strategic Combinations

Authors
Kent M Zimmermann and John E Morris

Managing director
Sian O'Neill

Law Firm Mergers: Lessons from Successful Strategic Combinations
is published by

Globe Law and Business Ltd
3 Mylor Close
Horsell
Woking
Surrey GU21 4DD
United Kingdom
Tel: +44 20 3745 4770
www.globelawandbusiness.com

Printed and bound by CPI Group (UK) Ltd, Croydon CR0 4YY, United Kingdom

ISBN 9781787428454
EPUB ISBN 9781787428461
Adobe PDF ISBN 9781787428478

Table of contents

Foreword

Peter Zeughauser
Zeughauser Group

In 1854, William H Seward and Richard M Blatchford merged their respective law firms, forming Blatchford, Seward & Griswold. After a series of name changes, in 1944 the merged firm took the name Cravath Swaine & Moore.

Debevoise, Stevenson, Plimpton & Page merged with Hatch, McLean, Root & Hinch in 1943, choosing to practise as Debevoise, Plimpton & McLean in 1947. After a series of further name changes, on its 50th anniversary in 1981 the firm settled on the name Debevoise & Plimpton.

In 1982, the partners of Hedlund, Hunter & Lynch, a 20-lawyer Chicago litigation boutique that had spun off from Kirkland & Ellis six years earlier, voted to be acquired by a 126-lawyer four-office California firm. For several years, the firm operated in Chicago under the name Latham, Watkins, Hedlund, Hunter & Lynch. Ultimately, the last three names were dropped and the firm now operates as Latham & Watkins. Bob Dell, a Hedlund associate at the time of the merger, was elected chair of Latham 12 years after the merger and led the firm for 20 years as it grew to 2,200 lawyers in 33 offices around the world.

In 2012 (30 years after the merger), John Lynch, a co-founder of the Chicago firm, was quoted in *The American Lawyer* as saying:

> *... if they hadn't [opened] in Chicago, I don't know what would have happened to Latham ... If they [had remained] a small West Coast–presence firm, I don't know where they would be today.*[1]

Would any Big Law partner argue today that Hedlund Hunter's decision to be acquired by a firm more than six times larger than itself was a strategic blunder that adversely compromised its culture, much less its future? Or that the Seward Blatchford merger and the Debevoise Hatch merger were failures? Yet for many years top firms scorned mergers for one reason after another – a sentiment that usually stems from the fear of losing or compromising something unique or different about their culture or becoming bigger for the sake of being big.

Indeed, all the firms mentioned above went on to achieve more following their merger and benefit from scale. For instance, with regard to culture specifically, Cravath turned its own culture upside down in 1906 when Paul Cravath created the Cravath model, based on developing talent internally and then picking the best to be made partner – a model subsequently so highly regarded that it was broadly adopted across the industry; one that endured and fuelled Big Law's growth for a century. And Bob Dell, who joined Hedlund, Hunter & Lynch out of law school when it was a litigation boutique, went on to transform Latham into a global powerhouse mega-firm.

Now comes this Special Report by Kent M Zimmermann and John E Morris, including candid stories told by the leaders themselves who have merged firms, about how and why they pursued combinations.

The common story lines of these leaders are compelling: to better serve clients, to take advantage of new opportunities as markets expand across regions and across the globe, to inoculate themselves against mercenary poachers, to bring together top talent to build a stronger brand and to fuel financial performance – propelling themselves onto the path to become the best in the minds of the clients they want to serve for the work they want most.

Why is it that the 19th and 20th-century success stories of Seward, Hatch and Hedlund are lost on so many others of the leading law firm partnerships of the 21st century? What is it that motivates partnerships to merge? The stories recounted in this Special Report shed light on the answers to these questions.

Building consensus to achieve a law firm merger, whether the merger is between two firms of equal size or a combination of a large and a smaller firm, is one of the most difficult undertakings of any law firm chair or managing partner. We see this in our work at Zeughauser Group in almost every combination on which we advise.

"Building consensus to achieve a law firm merger, whether the merger is between two firms of equal size or a combination of a large and a smaller firm, is one of the most difficult undertakings of any law firm chair or managing partner."

What follows on these pages provides invaluable guidance for law firm leaders desirous of navigating their way to a successful combination. Starting with assessing the competitive environment, the authors focus on the benefits of scale relative to a given market, focus on core strengths, building consensus among the partners around the defining question of what success looks like and cultivating a high-performing culture, all as predicates to success.

Kent and John devote particular attention to what is often a weak or even missing link in the process of tying two firms together: the careful selection of a merger partner. More often than not, predilections of law firm leaders and partners about which other firm would be a good merger fit for their firm are based on anecdotal impressions rather than research and data. An over-the-transom entreaty from another firm, or maybe an outward shot in the dark, is too often the sum total of thoughts given to a combination. Too many combinations occur without thoughtful consideration of the alternatives. Many carefully researched entreaties are rejected out-of-hand based on outdated knowledge of a suitor or a target. The authors explain how to avoid this trap by carefully evaluating merger targets and making research and data-based decisions.

This is not a publication about the mechanics of a merger. You won't find a discussion of how to choose a structure for the combined firm, analyse financial statements, combine balance sheets, reconcile capital accounts, integrate compensation systems and technology platforms, address tax issues or any of the other nuts-and-bolts challenges of consummating a deal. Those books have been written.

Instead, this is a guide to building consensus among partners on the benefits of super-charged growth; about remaining relevant, competitive and dominating markets; about finding the right merger partner; about getting the deal across the line; and about making the deal successful. It aims to frame the large issues that lawyers, both in management and rank-and-file, need to consider when weighing their firms' strategies and sensitise them to the human dynamics of mergers that make or break any deal in a profession that revolves around service to clients, pride in one's work and trust among colleagues.

Kent has been my partner at Zeughauser Group for more than a dozen years, consulting with top firms and many of the most talented managers in the business about their strategies and mergers. He has downloaded here so much of what he and I and our firm have learned over decades. Our work has included advising on dozens of mergers, many of which are discussed here.

Those first-hand inside observations are combined with John's observations from years at *The American Lawyer* and *The Deal* reporting on the strategy and practical challenges of groundbreaking mergers such as Freshfields Bruckhaus, as well as the larger forces driving the business in the upper tiers of the legal profession.

The result is a Special Report that I am certain clients and other law firm leaders will, long into the future, turn to as a crucial resource as they consider combining with another firm as part of their endeavours to grow stronger and lead the Big Law pack. At Zeughauser Group we believe that the 21st century will be an era of consolidation in Big Law, with a dozen or two top firms gobbling up the global market shares now fragmented among some 200 firms. If this becomes a reality, this Special Report will be seen as having mapped the path.

Acknowledgements

The authors owe a special debt of gratitude to Peter Zeughauser. For Kent, Peter has been a generous mentor and partner for more than a decade, sharing the insights and expertise he has gleaned advising law firms for more than 25 years on strategy and mergers. For John, too, Peter has been one of the most perceptive observers of the Big Law scene ever since they met in the 1990s.

Over his career as a consultant, Peter has advised firms on some of the most significant combinations – including several discussed here – and we thank him for securing and conducting several of the interviews published in this volume where he assisted firm leaders in planning and executing their mergers. In addition, he brought important historical context to the book in his foreword.

Kent wants to thank his other partners in the Zeughauser Group, as well, who have cultivated a culture of collaboration where it is deeply rewarding to practise.

We are also very grateful for the time and insights of the firm leaders interviewed here, many of whom Kent advised on key mergers. They were candid about their thinking at the time and the lessons learned with hindsight. We were struck, too, by a common theme as they spoke: they eloquently expressed their dedication to framing deals that would be fair to both sides and which were seen to be so across the partnerships on both sides.

We would also like to thank Michael Bell, our senior analyst, for his help compiling financial data.

Lastly, we are indebted to Katerina Menhennet, Lauren Simpson and Veronique Musson at Globe Law and Business, whose professionalism and efficiency improved this book and made the publishing process exceptionally smooth.

I. Understanding the flywheel effect

1. Introduction

Mergers and other combinations between law firms are nothing new. But as the pace of consolidation is accelerating, understanding if and when your firm should consider combining, and what a merger entails, is important for any lawyer contemplating his/her firm's business strategy.

The need for growth is one factor driving mergers. Most firms want and expect to become a better version of themselves. Their partners aspire to maintain or improve profitability, quality and culture, and to grow. As clients increasingly value specialisation and turn to firms that are known for excellence in given practices, sectors and geographies, firms must show 'bench strength' and quality as deep or deeper than peers if they expect to draw the most sophisticated, lucrative assignments. In addition, in a conventional pyramid firm structure, where partners are leveraged with associates and profit from associates' billings, growth is essential to maintain or enhance profit margins and to create continuing opportunities for ascending young lawyers – that is, to make room for new partners without reducing leverage.

Size relative to competitors in a practice or geographic area can elevate a firm's profile among clients and among lawyers the firm most needs to attract and retain. It is not absolute size. A 50-lawyer, single-office firm may have the edge competing with 20-lawyer firms down the street, just as a firm with 1,000 lawyers may have an advantage over one with 400. Studies have shown that name recognition of law firms is correlated with positive perceptions.

Scale also provides an advantage when it comes to pitching for business. Larger firms with higher-quality practices and sector teams can cite longer relevant deal lists, more lead deal lawyers who have mastered the industries on which they focus, more trial wins, more winning first-chair litigators and more relevant experience overall. To take an example, the bigger a firm's private equity and M&A practices are, the more likely it is that its lawyers will be able to advise clients on the range of market terms in current deals. The bigger its regulatory practice, the more likely its lawyers are to have a good read on key government officials and know how regulators are approaching investigations and enforcement efforts. A 50-lawyer firm with a strong 10-lawyer property tax group is more likely to draw that kind of work than a much larger firm with just a couple of specialists in that area, even if they are good.

In addition, many corporations today prefer to consolidate their work with fewer firms with more specialists and more relevant experience. Many corporate law departments have found themselves overburdened managing relationships with too many outside firms and feel that they get better results working with a smaller number of firms. This gives an advantage to firms with depth in many practices.

Not every firm needs to be a mega-firm, we should stress. Size, for these purposes, is relative to the market in which a firm operates. The relevant market might be geographic, a practice specialty, an industry or a combination of these. To sustain a leading corporate practice in a major financial centre may require hundreds of lawyers and overseas offices, but a top transactional practice in a mid-sized city could be built on a much smaller foundation. The key is a firm's size relative to its competitors – the firms with which it is likely to be compared by clients and the lawyers it hopes to recruit.

2. Some firms are pulling away from the rest in size and momentum

Scale is seldom a reason on its own for merging, but scale is playing a part in the evolution of the legal services market. Over the past two decades, larger, well-managed firms have pulled away from the pack in the competition for talent and clients. Their momentum is like a flywheel, which sustains itself once it reaches a certain speed. Whether measured by total revenue, revenue per lawyer (RPL) or profit per equity partner (PPEP), the 50 firms with the most revenue in the United States have put distance between themselves and the

"Scale also provides an advantage when it comes to pitching for business."

next 50, as well as with firms ranked 101 to 200 in revenue.[2] In other words, the market share of top firms is growing at the same time they are attracting more lucrative work and paying their partners more.

At the other end of the market, smaller firms that have outperformed their competitors have generally done so by focusing tightly on a limited number of areas of strength and cementing their reputations in those areas.

There is still a great deal of room for consolidation, even among large firms. The number one firm in the AmLaw 100 accounted for only 4.4% of the combined revenue of those firms in 2020, and the largest 10 firms brought in only 27%.[3] For well-managed firms, scale can magnify strengths and those advantages can compound year after year, measured in both profits and market share. Market-competitive annual rate increases spread across more lawyers than competitors is part of what helps a firm pull away. Once created, that momentum helps the firm pull away further from its historical competitors, often giving it an advantage in attracting and retaining the most talented, productive lawyers. As the practices and financial performance of leading firms become stronger, they also become more resilient – more able to weather regrettable departures and economic downturns, as well as maintain growth, even in highly competitive areas. That's the flywheel effect.

3. Compounded growth is a crucial factor

Take two hypothetical firms that have been viewed as competitors, with practices of similar quality. One's PPEP is growing at a steady 5%, while the second, which is more focused and better managed, sees profits growing at 8%.

Starting at a common base the PPEP differential is small in the early years – just 5.6% after two years. Over the longer haul, however, as the higher-performing firm continues to grow off its higher base each year, the differential becomes very significant. After five years, that firm would be ahead by 15% in profits. Even if its profit growth rate fell back to 5%, the spread between PPEP at the two firms would continue to increase in absolute terms, because the second firm's PPEP would be increasing by 5% off a higher base.

This is not just hypothetical. For decades, talent has migrated gradually to the firms that lead their markets in compensation, and that process is speeding up. Increasingly, the market leaders in profits tend to be larger.

As the highest-performing firms in any given market attract more sought-after talent, they in turn draw more high-quality, high-rate business, which supports further growth in profits and more recruiting. The flywheel effect works in their favour.

"It is not just profits creating the flywheel effect. There is also the less tangible factor of reputation and market position."

It is not just profits creating the flywheel effect. There is also the less tangible factor of reputation and market position. Firms that appear on an upward trajectory, expanding and drawing top lawyers laterally, have an aura of success that benefits them in recruiting associates and partners, and in the eyes of clients. Partners that are looking to change firms often see profits and RPL as key indicators of other firms' health.

As mentioned previously, scale alone is not a reason to combine with another firm. Combinations that are successful generally help both firms reach their shared goals faster. Together, they can double down on shared strengths to improve their competitive position. Each might have achieved that through lateral hiring over time, but that brick-by-brick approach generally takes much longer, has a higher margin for error on each hire and is very expensive.

Combinations can bring on more lawyers faster in areas that a firm has prioritised and allow for more meaningful due diligence about their practices. They can help a firm achieve its aspirations much more rapidly than expanding with individual laterals and small groups or organic growth. Moreover, combinations generally require less investment than large-scale lateral hiring because laterals typically do not bring their receivables for past work with them. Consequently, there is usually an extended lag during which the firm must compensate the new hires before any revenue is realised from their work at the firm. In a combination, the receivables and work in progress usually come with the lawyers, reducing the cash outlay for the firm they are joining.

In sum, a well-thought-out, carefully vetted combination can get a firm to its goals faster, at less cost, with less risk.

4. Within a peer group, larger and more profitable firms have important advantages

All things being equal, firms that are larger and more profitable than peers tend to have higher profiles and stronger brands, are invited to more beauty contests and attract more top talent. Nine of the 10 strongest law firm brands in the US, as measured by Thomson Reuters Acritas, were in the top 10 by gross revenue.[4]

In addition, the costs of attracting and retaining high-performing lawyers, investing in technology and deepening geographic and practice capabilities are also easier to absorb when spread across a larger and more profitable partnership.

5. The prospect of a merger can force a firm to address problems

There can also be other, less obvious payoffs to combinations. While they will not solve all problems, they often provide the impetus to

"Up-and-coming lawyers tend to be highly attuned to competitive dynamics and the market's perceptions of their firms and competitors."

address a firm's shortcomings. They may force a firm to move faster in counselling out chronically underperforming lawyers and they may encourage investment in growing areas of focus the merging firms share. Combining firms is also the occasion to look at the practices on each side of the merger, and to prioritise the growth of the best ones from each firm. This will enable the combined firm to become better known for excellence in its chosen areas of strength, gaining a reputation neither firm could likely achieve as rapidly on its own.

(Because there are risks with any combination – including the challenge of integrating a large group of lawyers and meshing cultures – it is essential to have a clear-headed strategy. We will return to management and strategy in Chapter II.)

6. The risk of doing nothing also has to be weighed

The legal market is not static and firms that do not keep up with their larger and higher performing peers, whether through a merger or otherwise, are likely to fall behind in profits, market position and market share. They may find themselves with subscale practices that are not as well known and therefore not as widely recognised for excellence in the marketplace. That generally makes it harder to win business and to recruit and retain talent to improve their position.

In the worst-case scenario, clinging to the status quo and allowing the firm's market position to slip may put the firm at risk. Rainmakers and talented, entrepreneurial younger lawyers – the foundation of the firm's future – may be tempted to leave for greener pastures. At other firms, they may see better pay, opportunities to work with more high performers like themselves, more interesting work and more promising platforms from which to build their practices. Up-and-coming lawyers tend to be highly attuned to competitive dynamics and the market's perceptions of their firms and competitors. They are also often in a wealth-building mode and are thinking more long term about what success looks like for them and what it will take to achieve it. For these reasons, they are the most likely to jump ship if they and other high performers at their firm question their firm's trajectory.

While many lawyers quite understandably would prefer to practise in a firm they know and where they can exercise more control, for the reasons set out above that is not always the path most likely to reach their long-term aspirations. Even healthy firms may find themselves drifting down in the professional pecking order relative to rapidly growing peers, vulnerable to the loss of top lawyers and lucrative work. The competitive environment in law is not fixed; it is evolving, with other firms scaling and increasing their strength and differentiating themselves.

For firms that understand both the upside and the risks, and have appraised their market position thoroughly and candidly, combinations sometimes turn out to be the fastest and most effective means to becoming a stronger version of themselves, building on their most profitable practices and raising their profiles. At the very least, it is in a firm's interest to understand the option of combining with other firms, the extent to which might allow the firm to achieve its aspirations faster and how to assess the pros and cons of a merger against the firm's available alternatives.

Pulling away

At the top end of the legal market, the largest firms have gained significant market share over the past two decades, as our analysis of *The American Lawyer* data in the chart below shows. In 2019, the top 25 firms accounted for more than 40% of the combined revenue of all AmLaw 200 firms, up from 32.5% in 1998.

Figure 1. AmLaw 25 share of all AmLaw 200 revenue

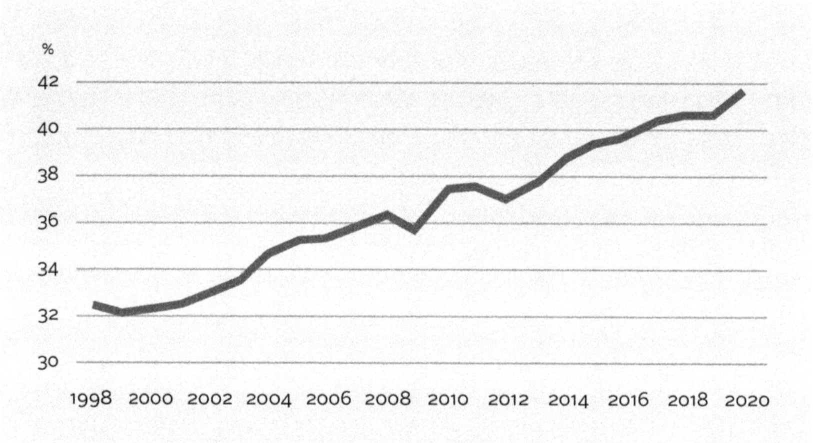

Source: Authors, based on The American Lawyer *data.*

Likewise, PPEP have grown faster at larger firms, as you can see when we break down figures from *The American Lawyer* into bands by firm size. PPEP at the 25 largest firms by revenue have risen more than twice as fast as at firms ranked 151 to 200 over that span.

Figure 2. PPEP increase by firm size 1990–2020

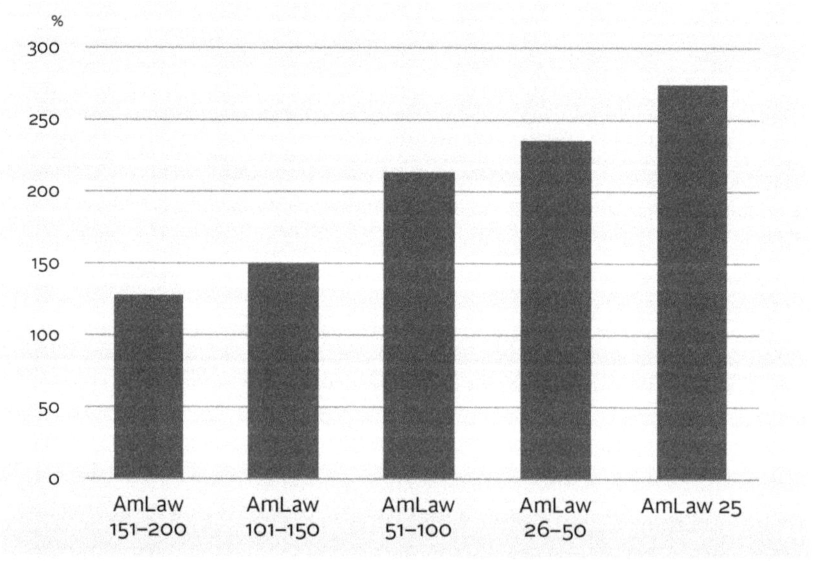

Source: Authors, based on The American Lawyer *data.*

RPL has also risen faster at larger firms.

Figure 3. RPL increase by firm size 1998–2020

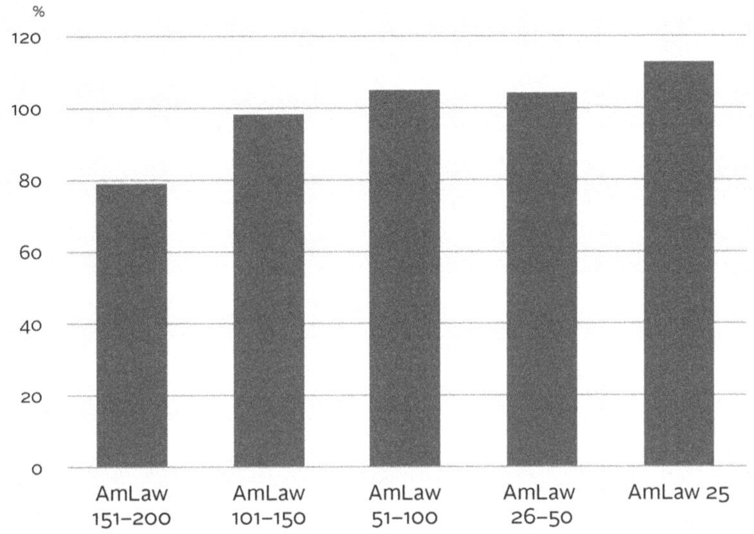

Source: Authors, based on The American Lawyer *data.*

Despite starting from a larger base, big firms have added lawyers at substantially higher rates than smaller firms, our breakdown shows.

Figure 4. Headcount growth 1998–2020

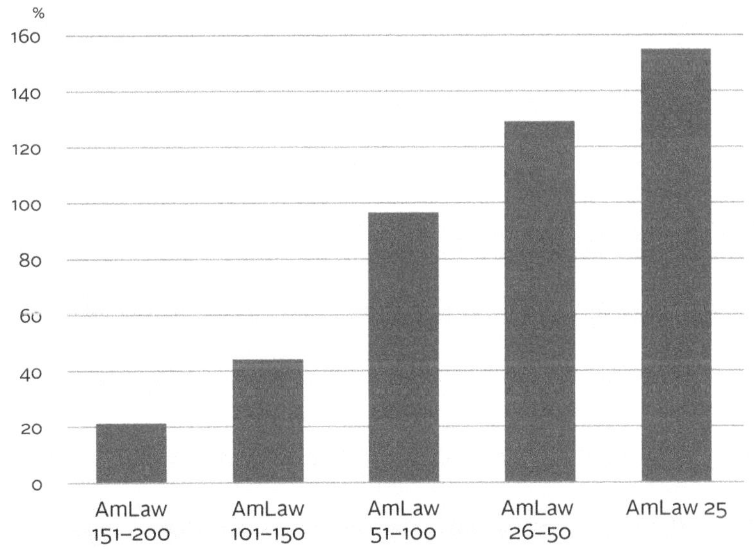

Source: Authors, based on The American Lawyer *data.*

Management perspectives

Law firm leaders discuss what motivated them to consider a merger.

SIDLEY & AUSTIN

In 2001, Chicago-based Sidley & Austin, with 925 lawyers, agreed to merge with New York's 400-lawyer Brown & Wood.[5] At that time, Sidley was well known for its transactional, litigation and regulatory work, primarily for Fortune 200 companies and financial institutions, while Brown & Wood had a leading practice advising Wall Street financial firms on capital markets, investment funds and structured finance matters.

Sidley had observed in the late 1990s that its investment and commercial banking clients were increasingly relying on their New York-based banker teams to execute transactions, and international clients were increasingly focused on Sidley's New York office capabilities. Pre-merger, Sidley had grown its New York office to approximately 100 lawyers, but the lateral partner market in New York in the 1990s was less active and opportunities to expand significantly were limited. Sidley believed that it could benefit from being both larger in number of lawyers and in the scope of practices it could offer in New York. Brown & Wood, meanwhile, believed it could benefit from both greater diversification of its practices and client base.

Larry Barden, chair of management committee:

In the 1990s, our firm had extensive relationships with many of the country's largest corporations. Two of our more significant and rapidly expanding clients at that time were based in the New York area: General Electric and AT&T. We were also beginning to build depth and breadth in the life sciences area, which was drawing us closer to many pharma and medical device companies headquartered in the Northeast. We had built a successful New York office, with substantial talent. But in the 100-lawyer range – with those lawyers spread across a variety of practices – we felt we lacked some of the depth necessary to capitalize on the increased opportunities we were seeing in both the New York and international markets. The lateral partner market in New York at that time was far less active than today and pulling top partners away from leading New York law firms was no easy task.

We had built strong relations in our Chicago and Los Angeles offices with the local offices of the major New York-based investment and commercial banks. During the 1970s to early 1990s, most of these Chicago and Los Angeles outposts originated and executed their transactions locally. In the mid-to-

late 1990s, however, many of these banks started to develop specialized execution desks/teams in New York. It was not uncommon to find that a deal originated by a Chicago or West Coast banker would be quickly handed off to a team in New York to execute, which often included the selection of underwriters-bank counsel. Thus, having strong capital markets and finance lawyers in New York closer to the banks' execution teams was becoming increasingly important to maintaining and growing our market share with Wall Street banks.

During this same time, we were expanding into Asia and Europe, and one of the things that was becoming apparent was that European and Asian-based clients – and lateral lawyer candidates – were increasingly asking, "How many lawyers do you have in New York – what are your capabilities in New York?" These inquiries also supported our belief that an expansion of our New York capabilities, particularly in some of our transactional practices, like structured finance, capital markets, M&A, would help us, not only domestically, but would enhance our profile and accelerate our growth in international markets.

By the late 1990s, Brown & Wood had also concluded that it needed to expand and diversify. It had become heavily dependent upon its capital markets and structured finance practices and felt somewhat exposed to the cyclicality of those markets. It desired to grow M&A and restructuring and build out its litigation practice. It also felt a need to expand its regulatory practices. Because Brown & Wood's principal clients were investment banks and investment funds, Sidley lawyers had worked opposite many Brown & Wood lawyers in securities offerings involving Sidley's corporate clients. We knew that Brown & Wood had highly specialized expertise in capital markets and finance, and enjoyed deep relationships on Wall Street. And we liked and were impressed by the lawyers at Brown & Wood we encountered.

The merger was labeled in the media as "Main Street meets Wall Street", reflecting the primary orientation of each firm's client base. While, clearly, each firm brought different practices and clients to the merger, there were several overlaps in our practices that created exciting opportunities for us to consolidate market share. We each had significant capital markets and finance-focused offices in London and Hong Kong, and our respective securitization/structured finance practices were both market leaders at the time. We also saw a mutual opportunity to establish ourselves in the rapidly growing Northern California market by building out Brown & Wood's relatively small office in San Francisco and adding lawyers in the Silicon Valley area.

FOLEY & LARDNER

In 2018, the 200-plus lawyer, Gardere Wynne Sewell, a longstanding regional firm originally based in Dallas, merged into the 1,000-lawyer Foley & Lardner, whose roots were in Milwaukee.[6] At the time, Texas firms were facing increasing competition from firms based elsewhere that were entering the Texas market. For two years after the merger, the combined firm operated as Foley Gardere in the former Gardere markets. After that, it reverted to Foley & Lardner.

Holland 'Holly' O'Neil, former managing partner of Gardere:

We were at an inflection point for the firm. In 2013–2014, coming out of the recession, Texas was becoming the preferred place for large companies to relocate. We were very fortunate in that regard. But, as large companies relocate, so do their service providers, and so there was an onslaught not only of businesses but of law firms coming into our market. Not only were they catering to these relocated companies, but they were going after what we had historically thought of as our mainstay, existing clients. That was the reality of being just a regional law firm when your long-time clients were becoming much more than regional in their business focus.

Most clients I talk to would much prefer a one-stop shop. The opportunity to be more of a go-to trusted advisor for those clients required us to look ourselves in the mirror and recognize that, just being a regional law firm, we were getting lower and lower on the rung, as it were, compared to some of our competitors.

We had also been trying to aggressively lateral hire to try to achieve growth and were having really mixed results. At best, lateral hiring was offsetting normal attrition, but it really wasn't growing the business. In addition, we were in a talent race, not just about attracting new clients or laterals, it was also about keeping our up-and-coming folks, who were being assaulted by the allure of more money and more opportunities at national law firms coming into our markets.

In order to keep even what we had, it became really clear that we needed to try to do a combination.

Jay Rothman, chair and CEO, Foley & Lardner:

There was the mirror image on the Foley side. For some time, we had identified Texas and Mexico City, and I had done some prospecting and spoken to firms in both Texas and Mexico City. We saw that as a hole in our footprint nationally. It's not just about geographic reach, but we also saw the booming corporate practice in Texas. We saw an oil and gas practice in Texas that we felt fit well with our renewable energy practice. We saw high stakes litigation because there's a lot more litigation in Texas that is actually tried than in a number of our other jurisdictions. We had a substantial intellectual property practice and we were looking to expand that into Texas. Finally, we had a sizable healthcare practice, and we saw opportunity there.

FROST BROWN TODD

In 2000, 180-lawyer, Cincinnati-based Frost & Jacobs and 180-lawyer, Louisville-based Brown Todd & Heyburn combined, aiming to protect and build on their positions as leading firms in their region.[7] Today, the firm has more than 500 lawyers in 15 markets in the Midwest and Mid-South, as well as Texas and Washington DC, focused on five key industries: energy, finance, healthcare innovation, manufacturing and technology.

Adam Hall, chief executive officer:

We had two firms, Brown, Todd & Heyburn and Frost & Jacobs, which each had, basically, one large office and several smaller ones. We began to see that the world was changing on us and, if we wanted to do the same kind of sophisticated work that we had done previously, we needed to get larger and become more of a regional firm, and we started down the path of a plan to have a combination between a Kentucky, Ohio and, later, an Indiana firm, Locke Reynolds, with a bit more scale to it to have the depth to attract that sort of sophisticated work we had come to enjoy. Otherwise, the world was going to pass us by and, to be successful, we would have to contract. From that point on, the firm leadership was pushing more regional growth between Chicago and Atlanta to fill in geographically this part of the country.

Later, the strategy shifted from pure geographic expansion to: "Look, we're going to focus on what we're good at and the sort of clients we want to attract, and breakout of our geography in order to achieve that goal."

Our expansion has made us more attractive to laterals – to very successful practitioners that did not have a platform of our size and scale that could reach new geographies, reach new practice areas – so we've been able to pick them up. Scale also makes us more open to taking strategic risks. It's a different calculation for us now, so we're willing to open a new office with not as much gnashing of the teeth and discussion within the partnership as we had at a smaller size, because it's a smaller risk based on our scale.

Robert Sartin, chairman:

Our size has also made us a safer choice for clients in our markets. Say you have to answer as a general counsel, or let's say you're a private equity fund answering to your investors on a particular deal, "Why are you using firm X?" The larger the firm is, the more it is perceived to be stable, and usually its deal sheets are a little longer, so it's easier to say, "I'm using them and they're a very solid and strong and stable firm," as opposed to, "Well they're the best firm in the area."

DLA PIPER

The firm is the product of some 25 mergers over more than 25 years. In the US, it began with the 1999 merger of 340-lawyer Chicago-based Rudnick & Wolfe and 370-lawyer Baltimore-based Piper Marbury. In 2005, what was then the 900-lawyer Piper Rudnick entered a three-way merger with the 1,350-lawyer London-based DLA and 380-lawyer California-based Gray Cary, creating a global firm with offices across the US, Europe and Asia. Gray Cary, originally based in San Diego, had merged with Palo Alto-based Ware & Freidenrich in 1996 and had built a strong franchise in the West Coast's technology sectors, as well as in Austin, Texas and Washington DC.

The original Rudnick & Wolfe/Piper & Marbury merger was driven by the need of each firm to diversify and expand geographically in response to the evolving needs of clients. Six years later, the three-way merger fulfilled Piper Rudnick's goal to build an international presence and stake a claim in the technology world. Gray Cary, meanwhile, felt limited without a New York or overseas presence.

Lee Miller, former co-CEO of DLA Piper, co-chair of Piper Marbury Rudnick & Wolfe and managing partner of Rudnick & Wolfe:

At Rudnick & Wolfe in the 1990s, we felt that you couldn't grow the practices the way we wanted and still have the quality necessary, and the clarity, to take advantage of the corporate trends of globalization, consolidation and convergence. The only really practical way to do it was by one or more mergers. To try to do it organically would, one, be very cost ineffective, and two, just take forever. And, on a quality basis, I don't know that you'd ever get there.

Terry O'Malley, former chairman, Gray Cary:

We didn't have the scale needed to play outside the US credibly. And, fundamentally, we didn't have what people outside the US wanted, which was New York. We needed corporate people in New York. I could go hire some, but I needed scale to be credible there. The practice at Piper Rudnick wasn't a perfect fit, but they had scale, and together we would have serious scale. They had 200 lawyers in New York.

They also had a substantial presence in Washington. We had a small presence in Washington and I knew we could sell Washington to the technology community. None of our close competitors really had a credible Capitol Hill presence. Piper had that piece. But, still, I probably would have been reluctant but for the London firm and its Asian practice. DLA had Hong Kong and a couple of other markets there.

"Before a firm takes any steps toward a merger, it benefits from having a clear strategy. That enables the firm to assess the extent to which any particular combination would help fulfil its strategic goals."

II. Designing a strategy around strengths

The basis for most successful mergers is shared strengths and shared aspirations. Combinations that capitalise on shared strengths are more likely to succeed than those where there is little overlap.

Aspirations here means more than hopes. It means a strategy: a reasonably achievable vision for the future with articulated, measurable goals and plans to achieve them. Before a firm takes any steps toward a merger, it benefits from having a clear strategy. That enables the firm to assess the extent to which any particular combination would help fulfil its strategic goals.

1. Formulate a strategy that extends existing strengths

A good strategy will begin with input from the firm's formal and informal leaders and rising stars about their aspirations for the organisation and what it will take to achieve them. It will also require an examination of data about the firm and an honest appraisal of the firm's strengths, weaknesses, opportunities and threats. Informed by these steps, the strategy will articulate a path for the firm to become a better, stronger, more distinctive version of itself. The strategy should exploit existing strengths and prioritise the growth of areas that improve the firm's financial performance.

Focusing on existing strengths – areas where the firm can be among the best in the relevant market – is the optimal way to establish sustainable competitive advantages and position the firm for growth and rising profits. Such a strategy will work to partners' advantage no matter what course they ultimately choose: organic growth, lateral hiring, a combination with another firm or a mix of these approaches. This is just as true for a 20-lawyer firm as it is for one with 200 lawyers.

A firm cannot become something it is not. At least not in one step. The strategy should generally be built around the existing practices, geographies or industry sectors where the firm currently performs best against the competition and financially. A fully developed plan may involve other elements – investment in technology and data analytics, perhaps, or beefing up the professional, non-lawyer management staff – but it should be based on the firm's existing centres of excellence.

2. Take a hard look at your firm

After assessing partners aspirations, the next step is to undertake a realistic self-appraisal. Where does the firm stand out in the eyes of others? Which practices command the highest rates or contribute most to the firm's net income? Which have the most depth, the best

"A firm cannot become something it is not… A fully developed plan… should be based on the firm's existing centres of excellence."

reputation and the highest visibility? The answer may be specialty niches, such as white-collar criminal defence or finance, or broader corporate, regulatory or litigation practices. Or the firm may be pre-eminent in serving particular industries or cities or regions. Most often, it is a mix of these things.

The strongest areas are, by definition, the ones that clients need and value most. They will also be the ones that will attract and retain the most talented lawyers. Sought-after lawyers generally want to be on winning teams in their fields and want to be paid what they could command on the open market.

It may seem obvious where your firm excels, but do not rely solely on internal perceptions. Do a reality check with clients. Interview them or, better yet, engage a third party to. Do the clients perceive the strengths, depth, points of differentiation and market position the same way as you and your partners do? How do recruiters view the firm? Ask next-generation stars about their perceptions. They are often the most keenly aware of their groups' competitive positions because their futures depend on it.

Before deciding which areas deserve focus and investment, be sure you are not harbouring illusions about your firm's standing. Reputations can erode and practices can be eclipsed by competitors. As in any business, long-time market leaders in the legal world are often slow to realise that they have been overtaken.

Financial analysis is also critical. A firm's biggest, most high-profile practices are not always the most profitable. For example, a large insurance defence practice or a corporate practice that efficiently handles commoditised projects may be prominent in the legal market yet not generate much profit for partners. Would expanding these large practices make a healthier, more profitable firm and allow it to attract and retain the most sought-after lawyers in chosen areas of focus? Perhaps – but perhaps not. If they are only marginally profitable, maybe they can be improved by counselling out underperformers or boosting leverage by increasing the ratio of associates to other lawyers. Only some number-crunching and thoughtful analysis will answer these questions.

3. Identify opportunities to exploit

It is vital to understand the firm's performance and trajectory relative to peers and against other firms that your partners aspire to be more like. This enables a firm to identify openings in the competitive landscape that it can *realistically* exploit. There is no point in a strategy that entails a frontal assault on a market leader that your firm is unlikely to unseat. Nor should a firm try to move on too many different fronts against too many different competitors, whether it is seeking clients or talent. Instead, it is essential to pick the turf – the practice specialties, locales or industries – where the firm can best succeed in the face of competition.

At the same time you evaluate current practices, try to identify potential growth areas that extend existing strengths – that is, adjacent practice areas. Check the firm's key performance metrics over time for relevant practices and also think about the future by considering what the essential trends are in the industries you serve and what those mean for future legal needs. Is investment increasing in those sectors and, if so, from where? Do they face increasing regulatory scrutiny or other crises? Are they spawning complex disputes? Where are the gaps in the competitive landscape relative to given sectors that the firm can exploit?

These considerations may shape which practices, sectors and geographies to prioritise for growth. For example, as private equity and other forms of private capital have become increasingly important drivers of M&A activity and control a larger share of growing businesses over the past two decades, many firms have built up their private equity, M&A and financing expertise, capitalising on that trend. Some firms have also combined expertise in particular industries with their private equity and finance practices to create distinctive cross-over specialties where they can be dominant players.

Another example: as corporate hacking incidents made headlines and cyber security became a priority for businesses, some firms prioritised the growth of privacy and cyber security practices to ride that wave.

When the firm has formulated its strategy, the analysis of potential mergers can then be viewed through the lens of strategy: would this deal accelerate progress toward the chosen destination, the chosen market position? The best merger candidates will be doing the same thing from their side and asking if you have a well-grounded strategy in place. (Would you want to merge with a firm that did not have a good read on its strengths and weaknesses and had no clear plan to capitalise on the former and address the latter?)

As we said, a realistic but ambitious strategy for improvement will benefit your firm even if you never contemplate a merger, and it will put your firm in a stronger position, with better options, if you do choose to combine with another firm.

4. Look for firms that share your strengths and aspirations
For a merger to work, the firms must be financially and culturally compatible. (We will come back to those criteria in Chapter VI.) But

"Where there are shared strengths [between the potential merger firms], there is more potential to create a combination that is stronger than the sum of its parts."

sharing strengths and goals is a very important predictor of success of any combination. In most successful mergers, each firm is perceived as strong in a number of similar or adjacent areas. This might seem counterintuitive. One might think that firms that fill in each other's gaps would make the best merger candidates, but in practice that is often not the case, unless the gaps are adjacent to existing practices. Where there are shared strengths, there is more potential to create a combination that is stronger than the sum of its parts.

Two extreme hypotheticals will illustrate this. First, imagine Firm A, which does only transactional work, merges with Firm B, which handles only litigation. Each would provide what the other lacks, but unless they share clients or an industry focus, combining is less likely to make either firm's existing practice stronger. Mergers where there is little overlap, or even adjacent practices, sometimes work, but they are much less likely to create real synergies – something more than their components. Moreover, they are often harder to integrate and implement successfully, because there are fewer overlapping interests to motivate the partners to build together.

Now imagine two other firms, each among the most preeminent in a major niche – say transactions in the healthcare industry. The two firms can create a dream team: a longer list of completed healthcare transactions, a deeper bench of lead transactional lawyers experienced in the sector, more relevant board level relationships and, more broadly, a stronger, deeper, more differentiated position of market leadership in the sector – a firm with a more defensible and resilient market position over time. Together, they create a magnet to attract top lawyers and clients. In the real world, most combinations fall in between these extremes, with some directly overlapping practices, some that are related but not overlapping, and others that have no counterpart in the other firm. The right pairing can still result in big payoffs.

The potential lies in the overlaps and the adjacencies, where combining related teams can create a more powerful platform. Consider a firm with a strong private equity and M&A practice in the software sector that merges with one known for the strength of its digital media group, including boardroom litigation. Because the two practices overlap, the firms are better positioned to grow and build stronger client relationships combined. On their own, they may be leaving business (ie, money) on the table without the other's capabilities. They are more likely to be perceived as a winning team, thereby capturing more market share with larger and more well-rounded client relationships, commanding hire rates and attracting the most promising and successful lawyers.

Another example: imagine an 800-lawyer firm known for its broad strength in the tech sector across practices. That firm is considering a merger with a 25-lawyer international trade boutique that has major tech clients but is not well positioned to handle non-trade-related transactions or disputes. Each firm might benefit, capturing additional work from the existing clients of each and more overall market share in the tech industries, while establishing more diversified, counter-cyclical client relationships.

These are just hypotheticals. The unique characteristics of the actual firms are always critical, but the right pairing can lead to deeper, broader practices for both firms and a more defensible position of market leadership.

5. View the issue through strategy

This brings us back to strategy. The key questions each side should ask are: would combining firms advance our strategy? Would we emerge stronger in the areas we focus on? Would we be better able to compete? Are we more likely to be a long-term survivor and a winning team in the market together? The more strengths the firms share, the more likely the answers are "yes".

The merger of two AmLaw 100 firms – Hunton & Williams, whose largest offices were in Richmond, Virginia, Washington DC and New York, and Houston-based Andrews Kurth – showed how this can work in practice.[8] They were each strong in project finance, but in different sub-areas, and neither was in the top 10 nationally. But they saw the potential to create a leading national practice. That single commonality would not have justified merging two large firms, but more potential payoffs emerged as the firms entered discussions. Hunton had an office in Houston, but it had not reached critical mass and it had made growth of its transactional practice and its Texas practice broadly priorities. Andrews Kurth, meanwhile, had only a modest presence in Washington, where Hunton had 150 lawyers. As talks progressed, corporate partners at the Texas firm came to see that they could benefit from Hunton's much stronger capital markets practice.

Over time, partners saw in detail how combining could benefit their own practices and fulfil their respective strategic goals. The discussions also convinced lawyers on both sides that their aspirations were in sync and that their cultures were compatible.

The most dramatic payoff came in the finance practice that prompted the firms to talk in the first place, where the merged firm catapulted to

"Over time, partners saw in detail how combining could benefit their own practices and fulfil their respective strategic goals. The discussions also convinced lawyers on both sides that their aspirations were in sync and that their cultures were compatible."

the top in deal league tables, allowing it to draw more work, boost rates and raise its batting average in pursuing clients, matters and lawyers. (See the 'Management perspectives' section at the end of this chapter for the managing partner's views.)

The same principles apply to firms of all sizes. A 200-plus-lawyer Texas firm that aspired to grow its private equity practice nationally and across industries recognised that an incremental approach would be slow and expensive, and that it would be easy to make mistakes while expanding. But, by combining with another firm with a high-quality national private equity practice that had prioritised expansion in Texas, both firms were able to fulfil key aspirations. The successful merger was built on a shared strength in private equity, and the combination allowed each to extend that strength geographically.

6. It pays to be patient

The best merger candidates are unlikely to come gift wrapped, perfect at first sight. Attractive features may emerge only in discussions, as the Hunton & Williams/Andrews Kurth case shows. The full potential often derives in part from aspects of the firms' practices that are not visible to an outsider.

In order to focus on the best options and not be distracted by the search for a perfect partner, it is best to develop criteria another firm would need to meet to be considered, then create a list of firms that meet a number of the criteria, casting a relatively wide net. If partners on both sides enter discussions with strategic goals in mind, they will be better able to spot those potential gains while also identifying and weighing disadvantages that arise. Framing the search around criteria will also make it easier to build a consensus later for a transaction. It will help partners become comfortable with the particular combination, and will allow management to answer the question, "Why this firm?"

Management perspectives

Firm leaders discuss how their strategies evolved and formed the framework for their mergers.

HUNTON ANDREWS KURTH

In 2018, the 700-lawyer Hunton & Williams, whose largest offices were in Richmond, Virginia, Washington DC and New York, combined with the 300-lawyer, Houston-based Andrews Kurth. The merger grew out of an established strategic plan at Hunton & Williams with both industry and geographic goals. The existence of that strategy made it easier to sell the idea of the merger to partners when it was presented.

By combining, the firms created a more complete energy practice and were able to address a wider range of existing clients' needs in that sector. Hunton & Williams, for instance, brought deep capital markets and finance practices to the table as the oil and gas industry suffered through an extended period of low energy prices.

Wally Martinez, managing partner:

> *Our view was that you had to be strategic in order to be able to be opportunistic when an opportunity arises. We had a strategic plan that we had deeply implemented about three or four years prior to the start of the merger discussions in 2017.*
>
> *Among other goals, that plan called for two things where this merger fit the bill perfectly: one, to expand our capabilities in oil and gas; and two, to enhance our presence in Texas. We already had a good-sized office in Dallas and we had a smaller presence in Austin, but not much of a presence in Houston. And we were traditionally seen as a power firm, not an oil and gas firm. We needed to cover both parts of the energy industry, and another gargantuan part was oil and gas. We've been able to build out renewables and we just brought in a nuclear practice, so we now have the four legs of that stool.*
>
> *When the time came to present this opportunity to the partnership, the partnership was prepared to receive it, because it was part of something that had been articulated, that hands had been stacked on.*

HOGAN LOVELLS

Today's 2,500-lawyer firm was created by the 2010 merger of the 1,200-lawyer, Washington DC firm Hogan & Hartson and the 1,150-lawyer, London-based Lovells, which had built a large network of offices in the UK, Continental Europe and Asia.[9] Each firm had been involved in significant earlier acquisitions and combinations, as well.

J Warren Gorrell, Jr, former co-CEO, Hogan Lovells and chairman at Hogan & Hartson:

Coming out of the financial crisis in the late 2000s, we were at the very beginning of convergence. All of our major clients were looking for ways to work with fewer law firms. I thought, "Gee, how should we best respond to that?" and it seemed that it would be ideal if we could assemble a critical mass of really high-quality lawyers with the right capabilities in the key markets to help address big multinationals' needs. We had a nice international practice. About 20% of our revenues came from outside the US, and we had some really good practices, but we didn't have enough critical mass in enough markets to take on huge global projects. We might have the capabilities we needed in London, but maybe we wouldn't have it in Frankfurt. Lovells not only had deep UK and European capacity, but also Asia.

POLSINELLI

The 1,000-lawyer firm, with roots in Kansas City, Missouri, has expanded through a series of mergers and group hires. The first, in 2009, when the firm had 300 lawyers, was with the 180-lawyer Shughart, also based in Kansas City, whose strong litigation department complemented Polsinelli's business and real estate finance groups. In 2016, with a growing intellectual property (IP) practice, Polsinelli acquired the Wilmington, Delaware-based IP boutique Novack Druce with 44 lawyers, which also had offices in Boston, Houston and Silicon Valley.[10]

Chase Simmons, chairman and CEO:

Geographically they [Novack Druce] were in some places that we thought we might like to be: Houston, Boston. They were in Silicon Valley. We were not in Silicon Valley. There was some overlap in DC. But they also had some other components that fit our strategic plan. Our IP practice was rapidly growing, but it was more pharma-focused at the time, and there was a desire to round it out a little bit. They had energy and tech clients. So, within the IP group, it fit a strategy of diversification.

FROST BROWN TODD

After establishing its position regionally, Frost Brown Todd's strategy turned to focus on industries, and five most prominently: energy, finance, healthcare innovation, manufacturing and technology.

Robert Sartin, chairman:

In simple terms, the firm first was focused on becoming a very strong regional firm, then more of a super-regional firm.

When I became chairman in 2018, I thought the future of the legal market was going to require size and scale and we had to have a strategy for that. We spent a lot of time in 2018 figuring out what our value proposition is to the marketplace, and that's to tell our clients that we know their business better than our competition, in certain industries. We did a lot of work to figure out those where we were truly middle-market dominant or, if it was aspirational, where we felt that was achievable.

Once that was in place, then the strategy was no longer about, "Is Michigan next because it's nearby?" Instead, it was, "Which markets are driving those industries?" So, it's not a geographic market for the market's sake, or numbers for numbers' sake, it's, "Which markets and which people help you in the strategy?"

"Apart from wanting competitive compensation, the most successful lawyers typically want to be surrounded by colleagues as ambitious and driven as themselves in an organisation perceived as highly successful."

III. The special perspective of the smaller firm

While our discussion has often focused on larger firms, the general considerations we have outlined are equally relevant to smaller firms. That said, the dynamics of combining, say, a 30-lawyer firm with a 300-lawyer organisation are quite different from a merger of much larger equals, and the smaller firm perspective deserves special attention.

Many lawyers develop strong, profitable practices within smaller organisations. Elite boutiques can be rewarding platforms from which to operate, and they often have prestige in the market. Partners in such firms typically value the independence and control they enjoy. They are often freer of bureaucracy, all partners know each other well, and the firms do not face as many client conflicts.

1. Staying small has drawbacks, however

The larger forces of the legal marketplace pose threats to many firms that are either under-sized and/or less profitable relative to competitors because of the following factors:

- Talent is generally harder to attract to a firm that is smaller than its competitors unless that firm is highly profitable and perceived to be among the best in quality and performance. Smaller firms may have highly desirable cultural elements, but the most sought-after lawyers usually want to be paid market-competitively, or very close to it. That can put sub-scale firms at a disadvantage. Firms that are larger and/or more profitable than their competitors can afford to pay more in general and, if they choose to pay a premium for a lateral they believe fills a strategic need, that cost can be spread across a larger partnership and revenue base. Apart from wanting competitive compensation, the most successful lawyers typically want to be surrounded by colleagues as ambitious and driven as themselves in an organisation perceived as highly successful. When sub-scale firms examine their talent flows over a five or 10-year span, many find that not only have they not grown the areas they wanted to, they have actually experienced net losses of top talent when retirements and other attrition are factored in.

- Higher-rate work more frequently goes to larger firms within a peer group, even when smaller firms are leaders in their areas. Without the scale to take on multiple large, complex assignments simultaneously, it is more difficult for smaller firms to consistently draw large, high-stakes engagements where the results matter more than the price. Also, clients are generally looking for a compelling line-up of talent, including next-generation stars, and a compelling list of relevant trial wins or deals. With the exception of some leading boutiques and other outliers, smaller firms tend to have less deep benches and shorter lists of wins and deals. This often puts them at a disadvantage attracting the most desirable work.
- Clients increasingly respond to specialisation. With the emphasis that clients now place on deep expertise in particular spheres, smaller firms – where lawyers often straddle several specialties – may have a harder time pitching for and winning the assignments they most aspire to attract.
- Clients sometimes have reservations about relying too much on a smaller firm. Clients are often attuned to the risk that their key outside lawyers could switch firms, or not have strong teams of associates or successors, either of which can be detrimental to the client's interests. When comparing firms, clients often see larger firms as safer bets, more stable and with the depth, breadth and name recognition that makes them more 'board safe'.
- Under-scale firms are more vulnerable to losses. With fewer rainmakers, fewer next up-and-coming stars and fewer key clients, smaller firms typically are more exposed than larger competitors to the impact of unwanted attrition or retirements. Clients may perceive them as riskier to hire and potential recruits may see them as riskier bases on which to grow their practices.

"When comparing firms, clients often see larger firms as safer bets, more stable and with the depth, breadth and name recognition that makes them more 'board safe'."

2. The cost of doing nothing is not nothing

Firms that are smaller and less profitable than their competitors in their market must bear these factors in mind and ask themselves if the desire to stay in a comfortable partnership whose members value their independence amounts to complacency. As we stress in Chapter IV about missing the window, maintaining the status quo may not be a viable strategy in the long term, and the failure to face up to these challenges can lead firms of any size to risk losing their best lawyers or clients, who may question whether the firm will survive or thrive in a competitive market.

3. There are tangible advantages to scale

Fortunately, corresponding to these risks are potential benefits that are often reaped by combining with a larger firm:

- Drawing and retaining talent tend to be easier within a larger, more profitable organisation. As mentioned above, larger, more profitable firms tend to have higher profiles and stronger brands.
- Existing client relationships can be expanded. Work from loyal clients that may have been turned away for lack of capacity or expertise, or which was never directed to the firm's lawyers, may be captured if a smaller firm's lawyers are part of a larger,

broader platform with more areas of strength and resources to serve clients.

- With the right combination, partners of the smaller firm may be able to attract higher-margin work. Partners that move their practices to larger platforms often find they are in the running for assignments they never had a chance at before, both from existing clients and new ones. Consequently, lawyers with strong niche practices often find that they can grow bigger, better-resourced, more interesting practices and be better compensated within a larger firm.
- Clients often reward lawyers who take their practices to larger firms. Clients who had concerns about sending too much work to lawyers at smaller firms are often willing to direct more business to the same lawyers when they operate from a firm with more scale, depth, capabilities and perceived stability.
- Typically, bigger firms have deeper management structures that allow partners to focus on their practices. Many partners in smaller firms find themselves burdened with management tasks. Joining a larger firm can free up high-performing lawyers to do what they are trained to do – practise law. A larger organisation can afford to invest in stronger management, by both partners and professional staff. Business development departments can

"Clients who had concerns about sending too much work to lawyers at smaller firms are often willing to direct more business to the same lawyers when they operate from a firm with more scale, depth, capabilities and perceived stability."

perform research and organise pitches, and data and analytics professionals can better inform choices about pricing decisions. In addition, the financial ability to attract and retain high-quality associates as compensation expectations rise can also provide more partner leverage. These factors all put partners in a better position to focus on clients and work.

4. How to begin evaluating the option

Here are some questions to ask yourself if you practise in a smaller firm and wonder about the merits of moving your practice to a larger organisation:

- Do you or your partners feel that you are at risk of losing talent? Are you able to attract the laterals you most desire? If prospective hires declined your offers, where did they go?
- How much more business could you attract if you practised within a firm with a higher profile in the market, as well as more depth and breadth – including in your main areas of focus? Think specifically about what you might gain practising within firms you admire and would consider combining with.
- Have you had to turn away projects that were too big or required specialists you do not have?
- Talk to clients. Would they send more business your way if you practised on a platform with a longer roster of high-quality lawyers and more name recognition?
- Do you get enough opportunities to compete for the most desirable clients and lawyers, and is your success rate high enough when you do?
- What is the draw of being small? Does that outweigh the advantages of practising on a more competitive and resilient platform with a high-performance culture?
- What do you most fear about combining with a larger organisation:
  - losing the firm's identity;
  - losing collegiality;
  - having little input into management;
  - having to change compensation; or
  - being forced to raise rates?

Then ask: how could you mitigate those concerns if you combine with a larger institution? High-quality smaller firms whose rates are within range of larger firms are highly desirable and frequently have better options and more leverage than they realise when negotiating the terms of a combination.

Reflect on these concerns candidly. Are any of them undue? To what extent, if any, do they simply reflect a resistance to change or anxiety about uncertainties? Can those feelings be addressed?

5. What to do if you want to go forward

After reflecting on these issues, here are some practical moves to begin the process concretely.

The first steps are the same as they would be for any firm:

- Identify the firms that meet your criteria;
- Consult people who are deeply familiar with the market both in developing your criteria and identifying firms that meet them;
- Learn as much as you can about those firms based on publicly available data and private insights from people you know who are familiar with the firms;
- Research the key cultural attributes of your target firms; and
- Talk to laterals and others that know them.

If your firm is substantially smaller than your potential combination partner, it may be particularly valuable to talk to clients about what would benefit them most – types of firms, practices and specific firms.

Also, give thought to whether it is essential that all your lawyers are included in a combination, or whether you could accept de-equitising some partners, or other changes that would strengthen your firm and give it better options. Depending on the economics of your firm and those of the larger target, you may have to face those issues.

Consider, too, if the larger firm has higher billing rates, whether you would be able to move onto that scale in a reasonable period. Would your clients absorb the increases? Many smaller firms find that moving to higher rates on a larger platform is more easily achievable than they first thought. If you think higher rates would cost you business, would that be more than offset by new business you can attract working off the larger platform?

In later chapters, we will cover various protections a smaller firm may want to obtain if combining with a much larger organisation.

IV. Missing the window, or not

In a perfect legal world, there would never be any pressure to merge. Firms could choose to merge, or not, according to their enthusiasm and comfort with the concept. In the real world, for most firms there are better and worse times to combine with another, and it is important to understand how to gauge the best time – how to find your firm's best merger window. Negotiate a deal too soon and you may not be capitalising on your firm's full potential; you may not enter from a position of maximum strength. Wait too long and your choices could be more limited and you may have less negotiating leverage.

The best time to identify and assess the available alternatives is when your firm has maximised its potential in its current form, when there is consistent productivity across the partnership, your financial performance compares well to competitors and your trendlines are positive. Such firms make the most attractive partners, so they have more options.

1. Perform an honest self-evaluation

This is easy to grasp in the abstract, but determining whether now is a good time to consider a deal is harder. Here are some questions to ask yourself and your partners to assess if it is too soon:

- Are your financial metrics (RPL, PPEP, expense ratio, revenue

growth) within reach of the metrics of firms with whom you most want to compete for sought-after lawyers, clients and matters?
- Has your firm done as much as it can do on its own, without breaking the fabric of the firm, to address chronically underperforming people, practices and offices? Or is the firm too permissive and is dragged down too much by this excess weight?
- Is the firm as competitive as it can be on its own in attracting and retaining sought-after lawyers in its chosen areas of focus?
- Could significant contributors at your firm command materially higher compensation on the open market?
- Are high performers and likely next-generation stars pressing for changes in compensation or management, and would they benefit from more scale?
- Do you have enough rainmakers, lead deal lawyers, first-chair litigators and likely next-generation stars in the areas you have chosen to focus on?

These questions will help flag issues that need to be addressed even if your firm has not suffered the loss of valued lawyers or clients. If the answers suggest there are many unaddressed issues, then it may be best to fix as much as the firm can on its own and articulate a strategy based on existing strengths, if you do not already have one.

If the firm can make a lot more progress on its own on these kinds of things, now is probably not the time to seek a merger. It would be better to do some clean-up and grow strategically as much as possible, upgrading the mix of clients and work as much as possible, so the firm becomes a better version of itself before contemplating a combination. As the managing partner of an international firm who was eager to undertake a merger told us when we suggested his firm wait and take care of internal business: "So, you're saying I should drop 15 pounds and see a stylist?" Exactly.

If you have done the tough work to get your firm into good shape, you will improve your options and can negotiate from a position of greater strength. You will be able to enter talks with the aim of achieving your aspirations rather than avoiding a decline. In addition, if there is more you are willing to do to close a performance gap in order to interest higher-performing firms in a combination, it usually helps to have a plan to get stronger and to have made some progress executing it. Then you can credibly make the case that the firm's partners are committed to continue strengthening the firm, whether or not it combines with another firm. A higher-performing firm will be more inclined to consider a deal if its partners know that your firm is on the right trajectory with a strategy to improve performance, and not just pledging better performance.

"It usually helps to have a plan to get stronger and to have made some progress executing it. A higher-performing firm will be more inclined to consider a deal if its partners know that your firm is on the right trajectory."

2. Signs the window could be closing

Typically, it is much easier to tell when a firm has missed the optimal window to merge than it is to tell if it is at an ideal time for a deal. Asking the following questions will provide some clues that you should not wait any longer:

- Has your firm's financial performance been outpaced by peers and is the gap growing?
- Are you experiencing regrettable losses of desirable lawyers – top or rising-star partners, or promising associates – to other quality firms? Are they trading up to firms that may have a brighter future?
- Are you having trouble attracting the laterals you would like to add?
- Have you lost desirable clients, or are you having trouble attracting enough new ones, due to competition with firms that have more breadth and depth?

If the answer to too many of these questions is affirmative, your firm may be increasingly vulnerable to unwanted attrition. This is particularly concerning if your firm is under-scale relative to competitors. You may have fewer big rainmakers, fewer first chairs and lead deal lawyers, fewer next-generation stars, and the loss of a small number of these, even one or two, could compromise the firm's outlook.

When firms fall behind competitors they can quickly find themselves in a downward spiral, with major contributors questioning the firm's future. Some will vote with their feet, departing for other firms they perceive as safer choices. That can leave the remaining partners burdened with fixed expenses and sagging revenue and profits. In this situation, when clients become uncertain of a firm's future and the depth of its bench of next-generation stars, clients frequently start spreading their work around more widely, often without expressly telling the firm that it is losing work that it might have drawn in the past, or why – leaving the firm to see flat or declining client relationships.

3. Standing still carries risks

In short, there is a risk in doing nothing in a changing market, particularly when the market is rapidly consolidating and higher-performing firms are pulling away.

Just because your firm has been stable and has long held its own among competitors does not mean it will do so for ever. These questions highlight the downward slope many firms find themselves on if they do not tackle internal problems, strengthen themselves as much as possible, and identify and assess all their options. The danger is that the decline becomes steeper, as the strongest lawyers feel undercompensated or that they are pulling too much of the weight and want to practise with lawyers they feel more closely match their abilities. If this happens, your options for advancing to your strategic objectives narrow, and the risk of backsliding and becoming a lesser firm increases. You need to prevent that from happening.

4. Addressing weaknesses

We want to stress that, just because there are warning signs of decline does not mean you give up. Clear-headed management can arrest a decline and stabilise a firm, buying time to adopt a forward-looking strategy. Often it takes the shock of departures – key rainmakers, up-and-coming stars or important clients – to spark needed improvements. But too many shocks like that can imperil a firm and lead to its disintegration; so if the firm has not already tackled shortcomings when it goes into this stage, it is crucial to act decisively to correct the problems that prompted the losses. By acting early enough, and with careful thought, a firm can still right itself and find a path to improve, whether that involves assessing merger opportunities, a more strategic approach to recruiting laterals and groups, a combination of these approaches, or some other strategy.

Management perspectives

Firm leaders discuss the risks of falling behind the competition in a changing market.

FROST BROWN TODD

Adam Hall, chief executive officer:

Our original merger [of Frost & Jacobs and Brown Todd & Heyburn] was a bit defensive. Thirty years ago, as a Cincinnati law firm or a Louisville law firm, we could do very sophisticated work. We were involved in large hostile takeover litigation, we were involved in big deals, we were securities counsel for large public companies. But if we had just sat still, I don't think we would have maintained that work. We were not trying to be an AmLaw 10 firm. We knew what our place was in the market and what we were trying to become in the middle market area. But had we not achieved the strategic growth we've achieved [through the merger], I think we would have lost the ability to get very good, very sophisticated work. And we were able to continue to do that.

Robert Sartin, chairman:

There are firms that may not be keeping up with the market and its rate of change. While they may still be in the market, they don't have the reputations they used to have and they're not doing the same quality work. To continue to provide our clients high-quality service, we knew we needed to grow strategically.

"Firm managers need to bear in mind that deal discussions are demanding and they need to ration their time and the time of the partnership at large so the best opportunities get the attention they deserve."

V. Taking the driver's seat

When a firm has articulated a strategy to achieve its partners' aspirations and has become the best possible version of itself – or has taken significant steps to reach that goal – it can consider mergers from a position of strength. The next step is to become proactive, to take the driver's seat in the process. To do that, management will benefit from developing a consensus among formal and informal leaders in the firm about what kind of firm would make the best match.

We stress the need to be proactive, because too many firms remain passive about the possibility of a combination. A chair or managing partner may take calls from other firms, or partners may discuss merger possibilities informally with lawyers at other firms that they cross paths with. Sometimes these can lead to talks, and even deals, but they are unlikely to lead to the best outcome, because mergers that bear the most fruit are typically developed and measured against the firm's goals and strategy. Finding the best merger options requires a thoughtful, well-researched approach and a careful prioritisation of potential pairings. A firm that remains reactive will often see only the more obvious opportunities, or those that present themselves by chance, or that fit another firm's agenda. Even if an attractive deal arrives this way, there is no guarantee that it will be as good an option as what your firm could achieve by proactively identifying, developing and vetting all available alternatives carefully.

1. Being reactive carries risks
Merger discussions can develop momentum and, if the starting point is wrong, momentum can carry a firm away from understanding and pursuing its best available alternatives. That can sour partners on the concept, leading to deal fatigue. Firm managers need to bear in mind that deal discussions are demanding and they need to ration their time and the time of the partnership at large so the best opportunities get the attention they deserve.

Firms that are reactive also can find themselves in awkward positions when talks get underway. Suppose that, after being approached and talking and exchanging an early round of high-level client and financial information with a merger candidate, a second prospect emerges (or is advocated by key partners) that could be a better fit. It would then be very difficult to put talks on hold with the first firm to explore the other option. Doing that would send a message of ambivalence or lack of urgency to the first firm. Partners there may be put off. If the second option does not pan out, your firm could end up with fewer options than it began with.

As a practical matter, it is difficult to be in advanced talks with two firms at once. The more talks pick up speed, the more time that a firm needs to invest in them to make them productive and keep them moving. That means time spent on assessing the opportunity; reviewing and evaluating data exchanged between the firms; and projecting the value of the combination to each firm relative to other alternatives. This imposes a large burden on management and other partners, with serious talks requiring an emotional commitment and intense work to reach a consensus on both sides. It is hard to do that with two potential merger partners at once. Moreover, other firms may not want to feel they are in a beauty contest, or that your firm is on the auction block.

2. Agree on criteria and frame the discussion around those
This situation can be avoided by taking the initiative, developing criteria that another firm would need to meet to be considered by your firm, compiling a list of potential candidates that meet your firm's criteria, and ranking them to prioritise the available alternatives based on how they would help achieve your firm's aspirations. Your firm's position, priorities and goals will drive your criteria, which in turn will determine the range of feasible options. This approach, unsurprisingly, leads to more positive outcomes than those resulting from chance or a call from another firm because your firm meets their criteria. It also ensures an orderly process where priority is given to the most appealing options available.

Reaching some level of consensus on the criteria for targeting other firms is an important step because, without it, agreeing on whether a specific firm is a worthy candidate will be challenging. From the outset, any merger discussion should be framed by the firm's strategy. The strategy is composed of an aspirational but achievable vision for the future and goals that the firm must meet to realise the vision. In the course of formulating a strategy and the follow-on work to improve the firm, management should already canvas partners about what they want to build together for the future of their practice.

If management believes a combination should be considered as a means to accelerate achievement of the firm's vision, another round of consultations may be in order. The consultations serve two purposes. First, they help leadership get a sense of support for exploring a combination and, if so, what the other firm should look like. Secondly, merely asking key partners about their views at the outset of the process typically makes it easier to get buy-in later for any combination that management ultimately feels it is in the firm's best interests to consummate.

It is typically productive to canvass both formal and informal leaders in the firm. Informal leaders include likely next-generation leaders,

"Reaching some level of consensus on the criteria for targeting other firms is an important step because, without it, agreeing on whether a specific firm is a worthy candidate will be challenging."

significant contributors and key opinion leaders who are not in formal leadership roles. Some firms have outside advisers conduct the interviews on an unattributed basis to help ensure that responses are candid. This can make it easier to identify common threads that run through the internal thinking of key partners about true interest in a potential combination, and what criteria another firm would need to meet to be considered. In other words, what practices would the other firm need to have high-quality depth in to be considered? What cities should it have offices in? How about the other firm's financial performance, cultural attributes and mix of clients and work?

At this stage, the consultation should be framed as a discussion of the criteria for selecting potential combination partners that would move the firm closer to achieving the partnership's aspirations for the future. It is important not to get caught up in discussing specific possible merger candidates too soon. The discussion should be about criteria that advance the strategy.

Inevitably, opinions about the criteria will differ, but the input from the partner consultations will serve as the basis for a more detailed discussion. Working with the input from important partners across the firm, management can work toward a consensus on the types of firms to identify, assess and potentially approach. From there, the firm can develop a list of potential targets.

3. Consensus on the criteria lays the groundwork for a deal later

The consultations are a first, important step toward participation by the broader partnership in the merger process. Combining firms is obviously a momentous decision. The right deal can be transformative, allowing a firm to leap-frog peers. But, inevitably, some partners will resist a move that will alter the status quo, particularly if there is a perception of uncertainty. Some will be resistant to any specific proposal. Involving informal leaders from outside management in the process of establishing criteria will give them context and a framework to understand why specific proposed targets are brought to them later. Management can explain how a particular firm meets the criteria developed in discussion with key partners. The process will reinforce the importance of making the choice within the framework of the firm's aspirations and the areas on which it has chosen to focus. It places the choices in a rational, analytical framework tied to agreed goals.

The discussions around those criteria will also help establish buy-in to the process and the idea of a merger.

VI. Drawing up the list

A well-researched list of potential firms will allow you to prioritise your efforts and avoid missteps that can set your firm back in achieving its goals.

You should invest the time, using market intelligence, to inform yourself about other firms so you have a well-grounded list of potential targets and can rank them by preference and feasibility. Focusing on the wrong firms at the outset can delay or even sabotage your plans.

As a practical matter, it is not possible to thoroughly evaluate and have in-depth discussions with more than a couple of firms at once, as discussed above. As we have stressed, talks and information sharing are time consuming and, as talks progress, they entail an emotional commitment on both sides. Human nature makes that challenging to sustain on too many fronts.

False starts also carry risks. If serious obstacles surface after talks begin (eg, client conflicts, a cultural mismatch, lack of a shared vision for the future), that can lead to disappointment on one or both sides. It can also create resistance to the concept of a deal among your partners. After too many dead ends, they may suffer from deal fatigue. Additionally, if word leaks out that your firm has had unsuccessful merger talks, that could create the impression that it (or the other firm) is ailing or is damaged goods. Other firms you reach out to later may also feel they are second choices.

Another big risk if word of a potential merger gets out is that headhunters may descend on the firms, hoping to dislodge partners.

For all these reasons and those discussed in Chapter V, it is vital to do your homework so your list of potential merger partners is the best it can be. The old carpenter's adage applies: measure twice, cut once. Use your resources wisely, particularly your time and personal capital.

Developing a well-thought-out list will also help management sell a deal internally if one emerges. If a recommended option is brought to the full partnership, some partners may ask why this or that firm was not considered. A well-grounded list will enable management to reveal the firms that were considered and the extent to which they met criteria that were developed, explain how the firms were evaluated, how they were prioritised, which firms were approached and engaged in discussions, how those unfolded and, more generally, why the firm recommended is the best available option to fulfil your firm's strategic goals.

1. Framing the initial criteria

The first step in creating a list is to articulate the characteristics another firm needs to have. Working from your strategy and goals, develop criteria for quality and market position in practices, industry sectors and cities that would advance your firm toward its goals. A size range is sometimes also included, since that is often a factor, but it is best to set that range widely. Much of this information can be gleaned from publicly available sources such as firm websites, trade publications and league tables. That can then be overlaid with private market intelligence about relevant firms, such as their growth priorities, culture and appetite to consider a combination and what kind.

At this stage, you are simply aiming for a broad list of possible alternatives so you can weigh the advantages and disadvantages of each. It is unlikely that any firm will satisfy all of your criteria perfectly, so be sure to set your parameters loosely. They should be broad enough that they capture firms that meet a significant number of your threshold needs, even if not all. Later information-gathering can narrow the list.

The first cut will also need to factor in financial measures, though those may be a bit rough at this stage. If you are seeking a firm that can accommodate all of your partners, you will want to focus on firms whose financial performance is not too far off your own, based on metrics such as profit margin, RPL, average compensation for all partners and PPEP. Although these numbers are reported publicly for most large firms, advisers sometimes have private insights on the veracity of reported figures, what drives them and what they may mean in the context of a potential combination.

Bear in mind that if you aim for firms with substantially better financial metrics or whose practices are of substantially higher quality, you may not be able to accommodate all your partners in the combined firm. That could make the proposal a non-starter within your firm. But in other cases, a merger may provide the impetus to tackle performance or quality issues that a firm has avoided confronting – issues that may need to be addressed in order to achieve the firm's aspirations, with or without a combination.

The basic financial information should be supplemented with other, critical information that often is not publicly available, such as the other firm's approach to compensation, capital and rates. You will also want a read on the potential cultural fit and what the other firm's aspirations and growth priorities are, and the options its partners are willing to consider to reach their goals. Some or all of that may be

"Bear in mind that if you aim for firms with substantially better financial metrics or whose practices are of substantially higher quality, you may not be able to accommodate all your partners in the combined firm."

available from well-informed advisers. Some may be available only by talking with the other firm formally or by talking informally with individual partners or former partners in the firm. In some cases, an adviser may approach another firm without identifying his or her client to assess its interest and its priorities in any combination. As you can imagine, without this kind of 'soft' information about motivations and goals, you may spend a lot of time in preliminary conversations with firms that look like a good fit on paper but with which a merger is not feasible for one reason or another.

Compensation and capital structures can be pivotal issues, and usually reflect a firm's broader culture. It can be challenging, for instance, to merge a firm that requires substantial partner capital with one that requires little. Similarly, it can be difficult to merge firms that use very different factors in setting partner compensation, or that have divergent views on what the compensation ratio should be from top to bottom, or whether individual partners' compensation should be accessible to all other partners.

2. Conducting the first screen

When you have framed the basic criteria, you can apply those to the universe of firms that might match your priorities, at least on paper. It

"If you choose to approach substantially more profitable firms, you should be ready to explain your firm's appetite to address the gap."

is okay to include firms that are aspirational candidates – firms whose profits or quality are significantly higher than your firm's – if you understand the consequences (eg, possibly not bringing all your equity partners in as equity partners), but it will be a waste of your time to include firms that are too far afield.

If you choose to approach substantially more profitable firms, you should be ready to explain your firm's appetite to address the gap. If there is a plan to do so and progress has been made, communicate that clearly. That may be the key to persuading the other firm to hear you out and engage in a more substantive discussion.

Similarly, if you choose to approach sought-after smaller firms, which may have been approached many times before, you should be ready to explain what is in it for their partners and clients and how your firm would be willing to address concerns that smaller firms' partners typically have about losing their independence and identity. There is often value in identifying and building long-term relationships with the leaders of such firms, in case the time comes when they are willing to consider a combination.

Once you have an initial list of firms that meet your criteria, it is helpful to organise the names in a spreadsheet, with potential target firms running down the left and columns for your criteria, so that you can quantify the extent to which each firm meets them.

Organising this information typically prompts more discussion and, often, modifications to the criteria. For example, while you may have focused on firms headquartered in a particular city where you would like to establish or strengthen a practice, you may discover firms based elsewhere that have built high-quality practices in your target city that did not initially come to mind. That might prompt a revision of your criteria and the way you are screening relevant firms.

3. Profiling the most appealing candidates in depth
Another good way to distil and evaluate firm information is to prepare rough *pro forma* financial statements and profiles of hypothetical combinations. Key projections could include:

- revenue, lawyers, net income and profits (combined partner profits can be estimated with a little maths);
- market position relative to peers and aspirational peers, using league tables and other measures;
- size and quality of key practices and offices; and
- clients of strategic importance and the potential to expand and deepen those relationships by combining.

This will help to flesh out the value propositions and business cases for different potential combinations and help you to prioritise firms.

Some questions to ask as you profile and evaluate firms prior to discussions are as follows:

- Does the firm have a history of mergers and, if so, how have they turned out?
- Is it undergoing a leadership transition (which could be either an opportunity or a problem)?
- Has it made significant lateral hires and how have those panned out? Has it suffered significant regrettable departures?
- Based on information available on the firm's website, in the media and in public company filings, can you identify relevant clients? Do your firms share any and does the other firm have other clients that would bolster your existing client base in sectors or geographies where your strategy is focused?
- How many lawyers do they have that are rated highly in industry rankings and in what areas? Do these numbers indicate that the combined firm would not only be bigger but would have deeper, higher-quality practices in your chosen areas?
- What are their league table standings like and what position would the combined firm occupy in shared areas of focus?
- Do any problematic potential conflicts pop out (eg, a policyholders' insurance coverage practice if your firm represents insurers, or generic pharma litigation clients if you represent branded pharma clients in litigation)?
- Are too few rainmakers responsible for too much of its revenue, are too many of them too close to retirement, or is business generation distributed more widely with a strong next generation of rainmakers coming up?

Be open-minded as you gather this information because it could highlight issues you did not consider when framing the original screening criteria. The process may well cause you to reflect further on your goals and opportunities. Be ready to tweak the screening criteria if necessary to eliminate some inappropriate firms and capture others.

Keeping an open mind is also important because good matches may not jump out on the first pass. The more information you have, the more potential there is to identify value to be gained in combinations that did not occur to you at first.

4. Prioritising your targets based on your criteria and feasibility
Throughout this research stage, and in building out the *pro forma* outlines, be on the lookout for value that might be created, where a

combination would achieve something neither firm could on its own. That might be a commanding position of market leadership in an industry or specialty, or in a particular geographic market, or a deeper relationship with an important client. These are the touchstones, after all.

With the data-driven *pro formas* and combined profiles, and the soft information you have gathered about strategic priorities, compensation, capital and culture, you can make an informed choice about which firm or firms to contact first. This groundwork will also supply the talking points so you can make a compelling case for an initial conversation.

"The choice of an initial emissary, whether a partner or adviser, should be based on who you trust, who would have credibility with the leadership of the other firm, and who is likely to have his or her call taken."

VII. The approach

With a well-honed list and your priorities established, you will be ready to approach one or two firms at the top of the list. Now you will have to decide who should reach out on your firm's behalf and what exactly he or she should say.

If you are working with an adviser, he or she may have already been able to make some preliminary inquiries to gauge the potential reception to your approach, as mentioned. If the adviser has an established relationship with the target firms on your list and you do not, the adviser may be the best choice to reach out in the firm's name, too. Advisers are often able to elicit more honest responses. Firm chairs and managing partners are often very polite to their counterparts. A leader who is approached and does not feel the other firm fits his or her firm's needs, or is not of equal quality, probably will not express those impressions candidly in a chair-to-chair conversation. If they are not interested, they may say that the problem is timing or with internal politics ("It's not you, it's us"). An adviser may be able to get a more candid explanation that allows the firm that reached out to determine if it can address the concerns and, if so, how. At the least, knowledge of the real reasons for a rejection will inform future approaches and perhaps even the criteria used to identify other firms.

The choice of an initial emissary, whether a partner or adviser, should be based on who you trust, who would have credibility with the leadership of the other firm, and who is likely to have his or her call taken. (From our experience, it is risky to use a headhunter in this role because they are often perceived as mercenaries and/or as fungible. Typically, they are not people who firm leaders turn to for strategic guidance. Moreover, we have encountered many situations where recruiters have told two firms that each is enthusiastic about discussing a potential merger with the other when they were not. That, of course, can lead to unproductive conversations.)

Generally, the first meeting between partners will take place with just one or two people from each firm, and perhaps an adviser to facilitate and help structure the discussion, if both firms think that would be helpful. An adviser can also give an independent appraisal of the discussion afterward, pick up on body language or other cues, and provide guidance on the next steps, based on experience with prior deals.

The number of people from each firm involved in discussions usually starts very small and gradually increases as talks progress. One of the largest and most successful mergers in recent times was pursued by the chairs of each firm practically alone for some period, because they had won the trust of their partners over the years and knew their partners would value discretion in a thorough exploration of combination opportunities. More often, firms have small working groups guiding the people involved in the talks. It all depends on the way the firm is managed and its culture. If talks go forward, the circle of partners involved will need to be enlarged with time. But in the early stages, it is best to keep the internal discussions within a very small group, because confidentiality is important. We will return to that issue at the end of this chapter.

1. Do your homework and gauge your audience

A partner who makes the first approach should be thoroughly prepared. Develop compelling talking points and questions that will elicit valuable information. Get input on these from others you trust. This is the only chance to make a positive first impression, so it is not a time to wing it. Think of it the way you would a pitch to a client or a sought-after lateral: be informative and persuasive, but listen carefully – as much or more than you talk – and inquire about the other side's needs and concerns. Your goal is to continue the discussion after the first meeting.

More than once, we have seen firms kill a deal before talks got underway in earnest by failing to do their homework. We have seen firm leaders go in either too confident or not sufficiently prepared, or

"A partner who makes the first approach should be thoroughly prepared ... This is the only chance to make a positive first impression."

both. An off-the-cuff approach may short-circuit the dialogue at the outset. For example, if a firm that believes it is highly desirable brags too much or suggests demanding terms, the other firm's leaders may see that as a sign of an overaggressive culture. They may fear that the relationship would be a constant arm wrestle rather than a collaboration. Or, if the message is not well tuned, the other side may be left with the impression that you have not given the proposal the thorough consideration it deserves.

As in any presentation, you need to calibrate what you say to the audience and the likely reception. But it is impossible to know exactly how you will be greeted, so your firm's ambassador should be prepared to respond to everything from open scepticism to serious interest. Build a decision tree to anticipate different reactions and think through your responses and their ramifications in advance.

Any information you have before the discussions begin about the personality and style of your counterpart and the interests of key partners in his or her firm is helpful, obviously. For example, it would be valuable to know before a first conversation if the leader of the target firm would consider a combination seriously only if the merger materially boosted a particular practice. With that knowledge, the comments and data points you share can be tailored to address that priority. This sometimes makes or breaks the discussion, particularly if the other firm has brushed off many other approaches. Similarly, if the other firm will reject out of hand any deal in which its partners feel they would simply be bolt-ons to another firm, and are adamant about finding a firm where they can create a new institution together, borrowing from the best of both firms, your pitch should be framed with that in mind.

In making the initial case for a combination to a firm at the top of your list, here are three basic rules to follow, as outlined below.

1.1 The goal is to get a second meeting
You are not trying to sew up a deal in the first conversation. Do not get ahead of yourself or hung up on details. Focus on explaining the potential you see in a combination, asking good questions and listening carefully.

1.2 Pitch the value proposition of the combined firm, not your firm
Your approach should stress the mutual benefits – how a combination could benefit both firms. This is supposed to be a win-win proposition, after all, so explain the payoffs to the other firm. Too often partners in these meetings spend their time talking about their own firm's

"You are not trying to sew up a deal in the first conversation. Do not get ahead of yourself or hung up on details. Focus on explaining the potential you see in a combination, asking good questions and listening carefully."

strengths. Think about what it is like to be on the receiving end of an unwanted sales pitch, or to be introduced to someone who talks only about themselves. That is how the other firm may feel if your pitch is all about your firm and you do not show enough interest in learning about what the other firm would value. Again, it is helpful to think of this as a client pitch. In that context, you would not want to just tout your experience and skills. You want to find out what keeps the client awake at night and then explain how your firm can help. The second approach is almost always more effective.

Show, in particular, that you have researched the proposition. This can be flattering to the other firm and often leads to more specific and compelling examples about the benefits of combining, which in turn often leads to a better conversation and more interest in continuing talks. To do this, point out what you know about the other firm, and set out how you think your firm could help the other firm achieve its aspirations, and vice versa. Share concrete examples where you think the firms are leaving money on the table, where together they would be more likely to attract sought-after clients, matters and lawyers that neither firm would be likely to draw on its own. If the other firm, say, is well known for its litigation and regulatory expertise in a specific industry and your firm has a strong transactional practice in that industry, explain the power of coming together to gain market share with existing and prospective clients, and build a higher profile in that industry. Or if your firm ranks number 15 in a league table in an area of focus and the other firm is number 20, show how together you would catapult into the top 10, establishing your combined firm as a national or global leader in the area, and how that could get the combined firm invited to more beauty contests and make it more attractive to the best lateral candidates in the field. If you share clients, explain why a merger would benefit them and make them more likely to send additional business.

In sum, instead of just advertising your firm's strengths, demonstrate how strategic you and your partners are, how seriously they take this matter, how much time you have spent learning about the other firm, and why that firm is at the top of your list. The other firm is going to want to hear why one plus one is more than two. Have good answers. Above all else, show how the partners and clients of both firms will be better off with the firms coming together than if they remain separate. Back it up with data and examples where you can.

1.3 Be sure to ask good questions

This is not just a sales pitch. In early meetings, it is typical for each side to do some 'buying' and some 'selling' – taking in what the other side has to offer as well as promoting their own firm. Keep in mind that wherever the talks go, meetings with other firm leaders are always an excellent intelligence-gathering opportunity, and an opportunity to start a long-term relationship. Here is your chance to glean non-public information – most crucially, the other firm's goals and strategies. The other firm may not have articulated those publicly in any detail. The more questions you ask and the more you listen, the more information you will have to build and evaluate the business case for a potential combination. You will also be able to compare it with alternatives, and it will give you a chance to address upfront any reservations the other side may have. Whether or not there are further discussions, you will know more about the competition and the market. Even firms with good competitive intelligence functions rarely have detailed insights into the strategic thinking of other firms. Also, the more conversations like these a chair or managing partner has, the more effective he or she will become in them.

Asking questions and listening also sends the message that you are attuned to the other firm's needs – that your firm is the type that could collaborate to make a merger come together and succeed. It telegraphs to the other firm's leadership how you evaluate opportunities carefully and manage your firm strategically.

2. Dealing with the sceptics

What if the other firm shows little interest in a merger, at least not with your firm? Here are two possible strategies if you expect that a merger proposal would be brushed off initially.

2.1 The soft sell

Suppose you know that the other firm has rejected other approaches; partners there have said they want to remain independent. Assuming that a merger is not an urgent matter for your firm and that you can be patient, one option is to take a very soft approach. Your chair or managing partner might simply reach out to his or her counterpart and say he or she would like to meet to exchange introductions and build a relationship. You can (honestly) say that you are aware of the other firm's strengths and you see some similarities, and you would welcome the opportunity to get to know each other and share experiences. Top managers, whether in law firms or businesses, often find their positions lonely. For that reason, many chairs and managing partners have friendships or collegial relations with people in the same position at other firms, even local competitors. They compare best practices and trade thoughts about difficult professional and practice issues. Such relationships are common, so the call should not be that out of the ordinary.

Your representative might mention that your firm has thought a merger could be the best way to fulfil its aspirations, and you have thought that there might be potential synergies in combining your two firms. Cite common clients or adjacent practices – whatever points of dovetailing you have identified. This could be prefaced by saying, "I gather you're not interested in a combination"; you are just interested to hear his or her reaction to the idea. Ask why they have rejected other proposed mergers. Learn about their growth priorities.

Obviously, the tone and content will depend on the personalities and the response you get. If it appears that even floating the abstract idea might sour the conversation, you may still benefit from an honest, thoughtful conversation about the challenges of management; you might establish a valuable professional relationship.

Moreover, circumstances change. For any number of reasons, a firm that is fiercely independent for a very long time may become more open to combining. Firms are proudly independent until they are not. You want to be top of mind if and when a shift occurs, and you want the other firm to think highly of you. In the best of all worlds, the outreach may establish a relationship and sow the seeds of a deal – or at least win you a hearing – down the road. If that is what you are hoping for, though, you will need to follow up a couple of times a year to make sure you are in the forefront of the other firm's thoughts. The message to send each time you follow-up should be something along

"Firms are proudly independent until they are not."

the lines of: "We know you are probably happy as you are, but you and your partners remain on our radar and if anything ever changes, we hope you will call us."

2.2 Enlisting client support

If you are unlikely to persuade the other firm on your own, talk to common clients. Sound them out to see if they would support combining your firms. We know of multiple cases where a boutique and larger firms have both done substantial work for the same Fortune 500 company and the larger firm was interested in a merger but the smaller firm was reluctant to combine with a bigger organisation. In a number of those situations, the larger firm consulted in-house lawyers and executives at shared clients, who supported the idea. Often, the work the clients send to boutiques is related to work done by the larger firms, and often the client feels it would get better results and service from a single firm. In addition, more generally, many large companies are working to reduce the number of outside firms they use. Lastly, in-house lawyers sometimes worry that boutiques and other smaller firms are vulnerable to partner departures. Clients dread the thought that valued specialist teams might scatter to new firms gradually or all at once.

If you are the larger firm, you may want to consider this approach. If an important client tells the smaller firm it should at least discuss the possibility of combining, you are more likely to get a foot in the door.

"Have a plan in case word of talks gets out. Have the outline of a press release drafted."

3. Keeping quiet and preparing for leaks

A few words about the importance of keeping your outreach confidential.

As we discussed in Chapter VI, no one benefits if word of merger talks leaks out. Either or both firms may be perceived to be in trouble, and rumours or media reports about merger talks too often prompt recruiters to descend on the firms.

Leaks can occur in many ways. Partners on either side who dislike the idea of a deal, or fear the uncertainty, may talk to friends, recruiters or reporters. They may also want to take control of their own fate by moving to a firm of their own choosing, which may reveal the talks to third parties. Leaks may also spur opposition internally. Also, if the talks do not come to fruition, one or both firms may look like damaged goods.

To minimise the chance that word leaks out, keep the number of people involved as low as possible initially. Do as you would for a client's merger: use code names for the firms and key people in documents in case papers are left out on a desk or attract the attention of others on a train or a plane. You will have to use judgement in deciding just how tight a circle to maintain, and it will need to be enlarged over time. For example, a basic conflicts check may not turn up conflicts between competitors or industries, or involving legal issues that could pose problems for a deal. Before talks progress too far, you'll need to consult with key practice leaders to make sure there are not any deal-breaking conflicts of that sort.

You should have a plan in case word of talks gets out. Have the outline of a press release drafted. You might say something along the lines of: "We talk with other firms as a matter of course and that is common among firms in our industry." You can be truthful while conveying that there is nothing unusual about discussions, downplaying the importance of them. (Bear in mind that the most important audience for your response may be your own lawyers.) Be prepared to talk to reporters on background, both to head off misinformation and to steer the narrative. Anticipate tough questions and carefully think through answers and their repercussions, too. Some firms anticipate the industry sources that reporters might call for information and reach out to those sources to arm them with preferred talking points for such calls. Also, have a response ready if a reporter tells you that key partners are looking to leave the firm because of the prospect of a merger. For example, you might say something along the lines of: "Partners come and go, which is common in our industry." Work with an adviser who has relevant experience to get your strategy and the messaging right if you think it would be helpful.

Management perspectives

HOGAN LOVELLS

Despite protracted talks over a merger that would span three continents, management at Lovells and Hogan & Hartson managed to keep a lid on their plans. That allowed firm leaders on both sides to present a comprehensive, compelling case for the deal to the full partnerships when the preparation was complete.

J Warren Gorrell, Jr, former co-CEO of Hogan Lovells and chairman of Hogan & Hartson:

We kept this whole thing confidential for 15 months. I just can't overemphasize how valuable that was. We had a core team on each side that was practice-oriented, plus some financial, tax and ethics people – probably 25 people at the end, but at the beginning it was about 10. That team did all the analysis, structuring and negotiation of the combination. And the same was true on the Lovells side. The standard for sharing information internally in both firms was an absolute mission-critical, need-to-know basis. Keeping the team down to only the people who had to know, and emphasizing to them that they had to be quiet – nothing probably helped us more in terms of ultimately getting this done than to have confidentiality throughout the project.

When it came time to tell the partners of each firm that a combination was something that we believe we should do and make an announcement to the market, we had really done all our homework. We were able to tell a convincing, complete story about why this made sense for our clients and our people. It was important to get that buy-in all at once, because once word gets out about something like this, every search firm, every law firm is coming after every one of your partners. Even your most secure partners get insecure when you talk about a merger, so there is a huge amount of fragility at that time.

Being able to keep this really tight for 15 months was so critical. Of course, it also helped sell it, because we had time to do all our homework and develop a structure and a business plan, so we had an answer to everything. Partners knew it had been studied and there was a firm-oriented rationale underlying it.

VIII. The second meeting and beyond

If, after the first meeting, both sides want to continue the conversation, the next step is to begin exchanging high-level information under a confidentiality agreement. One or both firms may also want 'no-poach' protection as part of the agreement, barring the other firm from recruiting any of its lawyers for a certain period, to head off any temptation at either firm to pick off the other firm's most productive lawyers. This is often a particular concern for the smaller or less profitable firm.

The point of the information exchange is to learn where value might be created by a combination and to flag up any issues that might be dealbreakers at the outset.

1. What to ask for

How much information you exchange after an initial meeting will vary with the enthusiasm the firms feel at this stage. You should not approach this as you would a document request in litigation. It is a first step in evaluating the potential for a combination, not a fishing expedition.

After a first meeting, the firms will typically exchange information such as the following:

- Material clients, however defined by the firms. Often the criterion is average revenue in recent years, though the actual revenue from each is often not disclosed until a later stage. For a large firm, naming 100 to 200 material clients is typical, but the figure would be lower for smaller firms. The purpose is two-fold – it sheds light on shared clients, industry expertise and geographic strength in areas the firms consider strategic; and it allows both sides to begin identifying opportunities where, together, they could more easily grow practices, industry sector teams and deeper, better-rounded client relationships with shared clients.
- Just as important, it allows each firm to run an initial conflicts check to identify any potential show-stoppers. Note: this may not catch some important conflicts, such as those involving issues that the clients may view as irreconcilable – for example, where clients of one firm have opposing strategic or legal interests to clients of the other firm, or take opposing positions in transactions or in court even though they are not actually adverse parties. But comparing client lists may well highlight the potential for those, as well as any out-and-out conflicts.
- Headcounts by practice group and/or industry and office. Some form of this is likely public, but it is helpful to have the other firm's more up-to-date, internal tallies.

"To really probe the potential, it is helpful to go down the list of the other firm's most important clients one by one before and during a later meeting to understand what each firm is doing for each client, and then to explore the potential for strengthening and growing the relationships if the firms come together."

- Revenue by practice group and, if tracked, industry sector.
- Measures of financial performance in recent years such as RPL, average compensation per partner, PPEP and profit margin. It is often helpful to exchange benchmarking data from third-party sources such as banks, although this exchange may come at a later stage if the firms are not ready to share this information after the first meeting.
- Range of billing rates by level of attorney, although this is often left till later.
- Proxies for quality, such as lawyers who are highly ranked in the *Chambers* guides, practices and league table rankings, relevant deal lists, significant litigation wins and corporate investigation engagements. Again, some of this may be public, but the firms will have more complete internal data. Some firms exchange their submissions to publications and companies that rank firms, because those summarise practices and people.
- An outline of the firm's approach to compensation (factors stressed and the process by which decisions are made), partner capital and a description of debt. This may be exchanged at a later phase.
- A description of the firm's culture, vision for the future and related priorities and goals, often articulated strategic plans and goals. This information is sometimes shared orally at an early stage and in writing after sufficient trust is developed between the firms.
- Diversity, equity and inclusion policies and statistics.

Using this information, the firms can build a profile of what a hypothetical combined firm would look like – a more detailed, accurate version of the *pro formas* you prepared before you had access to internal data. That sketch of a combined business is the next step in building the business case, a further articulation of the value proposition for the combination, and it can serve as the focus of the second meeting.

To really probe the potential, it is helpful to go down the list of the other firm's most important clients one by one before and during a later meeting to understand what each firm is doing for each client, and then to explore the potential for strengthening and growing the relationships if the firms come together. Likewise, with detailed information about the size and quality of the other firm's practices, you can project the standing that combined practices would have relative to other firms that are competing for the same lawyers, clients and matters.

Once you get to this projection stage, it sometimes helps to involve, or at least consult offline with, practice group leaders and partners responsible for major clients. Give them a chance to spot the growth opportunities, especially where new business could be captured in areas where the other firm is strong. Involving another layer of your partners at the right time is also a first step toward building the enthusiasm and buy-in you will need in advance of a vote.

2. Start fleshing out the upside

It is important to identify the upside in the deal as a first step, leading up to the second meeting. Do your best to put the harder issues to the side until the upside is clear, unless the problems that surface are truly insurmountable. Lawyers are trained to spot potential problems and it is easy to get bogged down early on anticipating problems that may surface, such as conflicts or potential challenges in meshing capital structures and compensation systems.

There will be time enough to deal with the hard issues. If the research you and the other firm undertake builds enthusiasm, people on both sides will be more open-minded and willing to find solutions to obstacles. Even conflicts that look like dealbreakers may not turn out to be. If there are enough virtues to a merger, it will be much easier to overcome the obstacles.

In the meantime, ferret out areas where value could be created. As an example, you may discover that each firm prioritises growth of its New York offices and that, if they were combined, it would be one of the merged firm's biggest offices. Both firms may be striving to develop next-generation leaders in M&A and private equity. Or you might find that you each draw substantial work from the same Fortune 500 company or fund, but in different regions or practice areas.

A successful second meeting will be one where both sides have explored in detail what they stand to gain and share their ideas on how to achieve those gains and lay plans to move to the next stage. The more detail you can develop about the likely upside for both firms, the more enthusiasm builds for additional exploration of the deal, and the easier it may be to work through impediments that arise.

3. Develop a process and a timeline

If all goes well after the first two to three meetings, you should set a timeline for the next steps and calendar key meeting dates so that the momentum is sustained. It is easy for the firm leaders orchestrating the process to be distracted by other demands. Just as in many corporate transactions, it usually makes sense to start with a hypothetical closing date, often influenced by tax consequences, and work backward to determine what milestones need to be hit and when. In larger, more complex combinations, it frequently makes sense to delegate some of the work by forming small working groups to sort through issues such as conflicts, compensation and capital, marketing

"There will be time enough to deal with the hard issues. If the research you and the other firm undertake builds enthusiasm, people on both sides will be more open-minded and willing to find solutions to obstacles."

and branding, talent, and technology, real estate and other operations. Those can proceed simultaneously along parallel tracks.

The working groups should aim for best practices. They may want to research how other firms have managed their issues in other mergers. It usually benefits the combined firm if it borrows the best practices of each firm, adopting as many as feasible from the smaller firm, if there is a significant size differential. Regardless of the relative sizes, drawing from both communicates that the merger is driven by collaboration and is not a takeover.

4. Identify make-or-break issues and work through them
After identifying and elaborating the value to be created for each firm's partnership and clients from combining, the time comes when it makes sense to identify any gating issues and determine how best to address them. Common difficult issues include:

- the number of equity partners that join the combined firm as equity partners if one firm is markedly less profitable than the other;
- representation in governance and management;
- the approach to integrating compensation systems and capital structures;

- any compensation protection in the early years of the new firm;
- the combined firm's name (if the two firms are similarly sized or if a smaller firm is highly sought-after and has enough leverage to raise this);
- closing date and how any accelerated tax liability is handled;
- disparities in debt levels and any other long-term liabilities; and
- integration of real estate in cities where both firms have offices.

It is easy for things to run off the rails here, so we advise firms to initially broach their views on these kinds of sensitive issues face to face, rather than in writing or on the phone. That way you can gauge the response, including body language, and address problems immediately if your conditions are received badly. Before the conversation, you should plan for how you will handle various predictable responses. Both sides will be weighing the trade-off of the upside of a deal against the inevitable compromises needed to come to an agreement. In doing this, it is usually in your firm's best interest to be thinking a few steps ahead: If talks crater, what are our plans B and C, and what are the likely advantages and disadvantages of those deals, or of not doing a deal, compared to the deal on the table?

Timing is key here. It often backfires if either side draws lines in the sand too early, before both firms have fully identified the benefits of the deal. But if you leave these issues too long, after both sides have sunk a lot of time in the discussions, the other side may feel blindsided. It usually makes sense to get your deal-breaking issues out on the table soon after the upside for both firms has been identified with specificity. That way, perceived downsides can be weighed against the payoffs from a deal. Both sides are more likely to be willing to make concessions if the case for the merger is compelling compared to the alternatives.

When you do confront the tough issues, the rapport and trust you have built up may be put to the test. You are entering a conversation that may make or break the deal, so it is vital to consider how the conditions will be perceived on the other side. We know of one case where the preliminary demands of a sought-after smaller firm came across as overreaching and overly aggressive to the larger firm. The negotiators at the larger firm concluded that the partners at the smaller firm were difficult people and would never fit into the larger firm's culture, so they called off the talks. From their perspective, the demands were a window in the smaller firm's culture, and they did not like what they saw. In fact, the smaller firm was eager to reach a deal and tried to reopen discussions, but its aggressive tack earlier scuttled the talks for good. Its efforts to restart them were unsuccessful.

Indeed, in our experience highly attractive smaller firms that are approached frequently are the most likely to overplay their hands. They sometimes interpret other firms' interest as implying that they can name their terms, and they do not understand the perspective of the larger firms, and the extent of the other feasible alternatives they have.

5. Voice concerns and state priorities, not demands

To avoid any perception that you are giving ultimatums, consider framing your conditions as concerns or priorities to be addressed, or ideal outcomes to be discussed, rather than as detailed demands. This is an accepted approach to successful negotiating generally that avoids a hardening of positions over specifics and sets you up for a problem-solving discussion.

For example, say your firm is a 50-lawyer boutique talking to a 400-lawyer firm. Rather than insisting on one or two partners on the six-partner compensation committee, you might say that your partners are concerned that their interests will not be safeguarded in a much larger organisation and need reassurance that their compensation will be set fairly. That leaves room for collaboration on an acceptable solution to both firms. Keep in mind that you are not negotiating a one-time transaction, where you may never see the

"Plan for how you will handle various predictable responses. Both sides will be weighing the trade-off of the upside of a deal against the inevitable compromises needed to come to an agreement."

other again. Here you are talking about taking on new partners for the long term, where you will need mutual respect and trust, and good ongoing working relationships.

We cannot emphasise enough that your view of what is essential or non-negotiable from your side may change when you carefully consider the alternatives. It is like shopping for a car. You start off thinking it has to have all of the bells and whistles, but when you see the prices for each feature, you realise you can do without some. The partners at the sought-after smaller firm we mentioned four paragraphs ago realised too late, when the other firm balked, that they did not really need all the things they demanded. On the whole, the deal was valuable enough to them that they would have compromised on some of their 'essentials'.

In short, make your concerns and priorities clear, but let the talks play out before you give the impression that anything is non-negotiable.

6. Start planning how to communicate with clients
By the time you are committed enough to the concept of a merger to be hammering out details, you will also need to be discussing how to tell clients about your plans – in particular, how it will benefit them. In part, that is a practical matter of managing and reinforcing the relationship. But be alert, too, to possible ethical disclosure obligations you may have – for example, if a partner's compensation will be contingent on retaining a client when the firms combine.

7. Be flexible about the legal structure
As sophisticated corporate lawyers know, there is almost always more than one legal structure that can be used to achieve the same result. That's true of law firm combinations as well. Ideally, you want one fully integrated entity with one profit pool at the top level. But that can take the form of a US limited liability company (LLC) or, for cross-border combinations, the firms may need an alternative structure, such as an English-law 'company limited by guarantee' or a Swiss 'Verein'. For regulatory and tax reasons, you may need separate entities in some jurisdictions.

Whatever legal form the combined firm takes, your goal should be to find a structure that creates incentives for lawyers in the combined firm to operate as one team, putting the best players on the field for each client matter.

8. Think creatively
Approach the negotiations as you would those for a client, bringing to bear all the creativity you would to solve a client's problems. This is one area where it is extremely valuable to have experience with prior

"Your view of what is essential or non-negotiable from your side may change when you carefully consider the alternatives. It is like shopping for a car. You start off thinking it has to have all of the bells and whistles, but when you see the prices for each feature, you realise you can do without some."

law firm combinations, or have an adviser who does, so you do not have to reinvent the wheel.

For example, the problem of integrating compensation systems occurs in most deals, and there are time-tested solutions. Specifically, it is common in large combinations to have a period of integration, often lasting one to three years, during which each firm continues to compensate its lawyers as it had on its own, but converging toward each other. Or if there is a shared desire to integrate compensation more rapidly and one firm is smaller, sometimes there is a compensation guarantee – a floor – for some or all equity partners for a time, provided certain revenue or other targets are met.

Discrepancies in partner capital can be addressed over time so that any pay-ins required can be financed, avoiding large financial sacrifices.

The combined firm's name can be a sticking point. A frequent compromise is to add the smaller firm's name for several years, after which the combined firm will revert to the larger firm's name(s), which typically come first. Since most firms with more than two names are usually referred to by the first one or two names, it costs the larger firm little to be generous on this point. In practice, the firm will continue to be referred to as it has been, but the smaller firm will be able to communicate continuity to its lawyers and clients. In larger mergers of equals, sometimes it makes sense to migrate to a new name that borrows from both firms.

Corporate acquirers often adopt some variant of this technique, using a combined name for a transition period to reassure the targets employees and to convey to customers that the target is now part of the acquirer. United Airlines used a twist on this when it absorbed Continental Airlines in 2010, retaining the United name but adopting Continental's logo, typeface and colours. Some law firms have taken a similar approach in their combinations.

Where the name issue is not easily finessed, we sometimes recommend engaging a neutral branding expert who can weigh in on the combined firm's best interests, given its strategy and the relative brand strengths and market perceptions. This consultant's recommendation can be valuable in breaking logjams. The cost can be significant, and the evaluation takes time, but it informs the decision with expertise and data, making it less of a battle of egos.

A variety of transitional measures can be useful to clinch a deal and ensure it is a success, not just in compensation or the name. In the complex, cross-border combination of Lovells and Hogan & Hartson, two very large firms, it was agreed to have co-heads of the firm for three years, one from each side, and co-heads of most major practice groups that existed on both sides. That not only reassured partners on each side that their voices would be heard; it also facilitated integration of the practices. (See the Management perspectives section opposite.)

9. Avoid flipping a switch that will leave someone in the dark
Whether it is an issue of money or leadership or the firm's name, the more you can avoid abrupt detrimental change for partners and others on either side, the more likely you are to win your partners' assent to a deal, and the more likely the combination will succeed over time.

Management perspectives

Firm leaders discuss how they worked through potentially thorny issues with their prospective merger partners.

HUNTON ANDREWS KURTH

In negotiating with Andrews Kurth, Hunton & Williams looked ahead to the day when the counterparties across the table would be partners, the combined firm's managing partner says.

Wally Martinez, managing partner:

We at Hunton & Williams were able to show Andrews Kurth that we are a shop that really does work hard at purposeful collaboration and that's something that would benefit them. As we worked to structure the deal, I knew that if this deal went forward, I would shortly be leading the combined firm and we'd all be practicing together. It is important as you structure a transaction and work about setting up the working groups and sharing leadership responsibilities that you keep that in mind. You're not buying a car and driving it off the lot. You're not selling a car and saying, "Well, hope you enjoy it." We are going to be one. It is absolutely critical to always have that in mind. You want to have a good deal, but you want that deal to be an obviously fair deal, in all respects.

It's really, really important to make sure you build in time when you are visiting with the other firm broadly to have the right one-on-one conversations. Try to develop a deep enough relationship with whomever your counterpart is so they can offer you insight into their side of the house – which partners might be having some concerns about the merger, and their relevancy to the merger – so you can have one-on-one conversations with them. It goes without saying you have to do the same thing in your own shop.

HOGAN LOVELLS

Reaching compromises around leadership was essential to cement the Hogan & Hartson-Lovells agreement.

J Warren Gorrell, Jr, former co-CEO of Hogan Lovells and chairman of Hogan & Hartson:

Lovells had a governance system where they had practice group and regional leaders and a managing partner, and the firm was really run by the CEO and these practice leaders. All of them were elected by the partners. They didn't have really any sort of representation from the partners. Hogan & Hartson had a small handful of people who really ran the firm, our executive committee and management group, with a strong CEO model.

When the Lovells and Hogan & Hartson teams stepped back and asked what the right structure would be for a $2 billion business with 2,400 lawyers around the world, all of whom need to operate together, we thought something as close to a corporate structure would be best. So we implemented a structure where a board of directors is elected by partners and a CEO and management team are appointed by the board. The board's role is really supervisory in the US sense, where it oversees management and the management team really runs the law firm.

So, more specifically, we decided we would have a board and we would have an international management committee (IMC). The board oversees the IMC. The IMC is composed of the CEO and the CEO's team, which has both a practice and a geographic focus and is selected by the CEO in consultation with the board.

In order to get support from the partners of both firms, we decided it would be best at the outset to have co-CEOs and co-leaders of the three largest of our five main practice groups: corporate, litigation, and finance. We had a single leader of IP, who was from Lovells since they had a preeminent global IP practice, and we had a single leader of our regulatory, who was a former Hogan person. We divided the world into five regions: DC, the rest of the Americas, London, Continental Europe, and Asia and the Middle East. It was a classic practice-geographic matrix, but practice had primacy.

So, the two co-CEOs, the rest of the IMC, and a finance person were the people who really ran the firm and made every important decision, subject to oversight by the board. Critically, none of that management team is elected by the full partnership. The CEO is appointed by the board, as you would find in a US corporation, and the management team was appointed by the CEO in consultation with the board.

FOLEY & LARDNER

Working together to forecast the potential synergies from a deal, Gardere Wynne Sewell and Foley & Lardner built relationships at the same time that they laid the groundwork for a later integration.

Jay Rothman, chair and CEO:

When we had the initial conversation with Holly O'Neil and her team at Gardere & Wynne, they focused on the same thing, and we committed to saying: "Listen, if we're going to do this, it can't just be happy talk around integration, it's got to be serious." It's got to be serious down to level of looking at individual client relationships and saying: "OK, you represent X, we represent Y, collectively what can we do together that we could not do independently?" And we really started that process in all the major practice areas, and a lot of people got to meet a lot of people. That was really helpful in terms of our identifying where we thought we had opportunities, and we had people that were committed to it and really wanted to make it happen on both sides.

DLA PIPER

Rapport and trust among the leaders of the two US firms that joined with DLA to form DLA Piper – Terry O'Malley at Gray Cary and Lee Miller and Frank Burch at Piper Rudnick – was crucial.

Terry O'Malley, former chairman, Gray Cary:

They had always been straight in the conversations that I had with them before. There was a refreshing lack of B.S. in the room when you were talking to them. Lee Miller was fond of saying we were the three tallest pygmies in the law firm. There was a self-effacing aspect to their presentation that really wasn't a put-on. We all knew, at some level, we were just lucky guys who were fortunate enough to have the confidence of our partners and a clue about how to run law firms.

These guys had also been through the merger drill. We had all started in the mid-90s running whatever law firm we were in at the time, we were roughly the same age, so we had a lot in common and a similar time frame in terms of looking ahead – how long we had in the rest of our career to get something done.

"Remind partners that the competitive environment is not static, and there is no guarantee that the firm or its business will remain as it has been. The industry is rapidly consolidating, competition for talent is getting stiffer, and clients are consolidating their work with fewer firms."

IX. Getting partners' approval

It should go without saying that you do not want to put a deal to a vote unless you are certain a strong majority of partners will support it. A defeat would be a blow to management and could make future merger proposals harder to sell internally. A slim majority would raise questions about how committed your partners are to making the combination a success.

Long before the combination comes to a vote, management should have been eliciting buy-in. Key partners should have been involved along the way, so they have helped spot and elaborate the benefits of a combination and support the transaction. Involving partners in evaluating the deal and, in particular, its potential payoffs, should have engendered enthusiasm in the ranks.

If you did not make a list of the partners whose support is most vital at the outset, now is the time to do so. This would include not just your firm's biggest business originators, but heads of practice groups (particularly those that are most central to the combination's rationale and strategy), up-and-coming partners who will determine the firm's future, and cultural leaders (eg, older partners who are seen as embodying the firm's culture and continuity and have its best interests at heart even if they are not major business generators anymore).

As negotiations reach their final stages and a vote nears, one-to-one conversations with these key leaders are essential. Management should hear out concerns that have not been voiced already, and to put the case for the ways the combination will benefit the individual as well as the larger firm. If you have not already done so, review with each key partner the top clients of the other firm and discuss how their needs are going unmet by the other firm now and could be satisfied by lawyers in your firm, and vice versa with the individual partner's top clients.

Very often it is useful to have management or top partners from each firm talk to partners at the other firm one on one. To counter the natural human resistance to change and the unknown, in these discussions and in group settings, be sure to discuss the risk of doing nothing as well as the upside of a deal – all the points we discussed at the beginning of the book. If you are convinced that the status quo is not viable, explain why. Explain that mergers are often defensive, sometimes to address the risk of partner departures that could change the firm, and those departures could include important contributors and next-generation stars who support the merger. Remind partners that the competitive environment is not static, and there is no guarantee that the firm or its business will remain as it has

"A few adamant minority voices are often louder than the majority, and they can dominate discussion. Be prepared for that."

been. The industry is rapidly consolidating, competition for talent is getting stiffer, and clients are consolidating their work with fewer firms. If your firm has slipped relative to peers in scale and profits, ask if alternatives to a combination really will keep the firm competitive.

It is usually best to begin the one-on-one discussions with the partners who appear most supportive of the transaction, because you can cite their support later with other partners who may have reservations.

As we discussed in Chapter VII, the more you can show that the merger will not cause abrupt changes, the more you will allay anxieties. This is where interim provisions to preserve continuity really come into play – for example, compensation or representation guarantees, or provisions to share the management roles.

1. How to structure a vote

Your existing partnership agreement likely specifies what sort of vote is required to combine firms. Some firms have a one-partner, one-vote system, but most weigh votes according to shares of the partnership, and most firms require some sort of super-majority approval for mergers. Regardless of what is required by the partnership agreement, you may want to consider going beyond that and holding votes on both a weighted and unweighted basis to ensure there is broad buy-in.

2. How to deal with vocal opposition

By this stage, you should be able to anticipate any opposition; it should not come out of the blue. Everything you have done by this point was designed to head that off. But you may not have convinced every last partner, and you should have a strategy to make sure that does not scuttle a deal that has broad support.

In law firms, as in life, a few adamant minority voices are often louder than the majority, and they can dominate discussion. Be prepared for that. When lining up support from key partners, ask them in advance to voice their support if there is opposition. If they strongly support the merger, make sure they do not sit silently in the face of attacks on the proposal.

Obviously, there may be genuine differences in opinion about the merits of a combination. But if a proposed deal has come this far and won the support of most of your partners, you need to ask if the opponents at this late stage are really seeking the best for the firm as a whole. Presumably the process would not have reached the stage of a vote if there were strong opposition from partners who are key to the combination's success – say, the heads of practices that are central to the merged firm's strategy.

In our experience advising firms, where a combination has widespread support in a firm, vociferous opponents often do not have the firm's best interests at heart. They may have fears that they will become small fish in a bigger pond, or will lose out in compensation or management, or they have some other motivation that is personal. That is not always the case, of course, but ask yourself what the opponents' motivations are. If you conclude that their concerns are not genuine issues for the firm as a whole, you may not want to give them great weight. Partners who are adamant at this stage are often discontented in various ways and may be more likely to leave even without a merger to prompt them. Ask yourself if you think they could ever be made happy. If the answer is "no", then you may just have to accept their opposition and go forward.

Put another way: do not let yourself be held hostage by a few partners if there is a good case for the transaction and strong support among partners. You should be prepared for the fact that some people may leave because of the merger, whether they speak out against the deal or not. If it is partners who are genuinely opposed to the consensus within the partnership about the best strategic direction for the firm, you may simply have to accept their departures.

Lastly, we should add that scepticism can help focus the conversation on why the particular deal is on the table – why management believes it is the best available means to pursue the firm's agreed-upon strategy, and how it compares to alternatives the firm would need to explore if the deal is rejected, including the risks of not doing the deal.

Management perspectives

HUNTON ANDREWS KURTH

Large groups of Andrews Kurth and Hunton & Williams partners met during the merger talks. A group of litigators that Hunton & Williams was recruiting in Boston was also brought into the discussions to ensure that everyone would see the larger project.

Wally Martinez, managing partner:

It's not just the deal team that's running the due diligence, right? They're doing the macro due diligence, as you would in any transaction. But every partner is conducting his or her own due diligence, and that is where being able to articulate how aligned the cultures are is important.

As we were going about trying to make this transaction, I spent just about as much time walking the halls and having partner meetings at Andrews Kurth as I did at Hunton & Williams, because I felt that it was important that they see me and other leaders in the firm, look us in the eye and understand that, fundamentally, how we look at our partners and support our partners' practices is very, very similar.

We had a number of meetings where we flew in a dozen or two Hunton & Williams partners to meet with folks from Andrews Kurth, and they did the same thing with us, and met at different offices. Of course, there were presentations and discussions, but there was a lot of time baked in for folks to meet face to face – the old look-em-in-the-eye and let me take the measure of these folks.

Plus, we made sure that people who had joined Hunton & Williams as part of larger groups were still able to tell their story, because nothing makes the case better than someone who came in as part of a very large group – how they felt supported and what it had done for them and their practice.

As we were doing the Andrews Kurth merger, we were opening an office in Boston and acquiring an entire litigation practice there, so we had some of the Boston people meet with some of the Andrews Kurth people, even with us not around. To really convey that we're all in this together, we wanted to get Andrews Kurth's view of this, and even the Boston folks' views of Andrews Kurth.

"With the right lead-up, partners should go into the merger enthusiastic about the potential to achieve their personal professional aspirations and build a better, more resilient firm – enthusiasm that is an enormous resource to draw on."

X. Making the deal a success

Our focus has been on getting the merger process going and approaching it systematically so you can find the best merger partner or partners and negotiate the best deal to more rapidly advance toward your firm's strategic goals.

If you have thoroughly vetted the combination and have worked closely with partners from the other firm to identify the potential payoffs, you will already have a head-start on an effective post-merger plan to release value from the deal as quickly as possible, along with fresh business development plans and management structures. You will have lists of clients and types of work to target jointly, playing off the new combined strengths, you will have thought through the financial incentives and goals you will need to set to achieve the aims of the combination, and you will have made plans for integration to get off to a strong start as one firm.

With the right lead-up, partners should go into the merger enthusiastic about the potential to achieve their personal professional aspirations and build a better, more resilient firm – enthusiasm that is an enormous resource to draw on. Partners often report that, to their surprise, the process of thinking about the potential of a combination is invigorating – the process encourages them to think about their long-term goals and how they can work together to achieve them.

But here are some specific suggestions that will help the merged firm realise the benefits the research and negotiations identified.

1. Frame a shared strategy
By negotiating the merger, the firms together will have set a shared strategy, but now is the time to memorialise it if that has not been done, and to set achievable, measurable goals. That will help keep partners on the same page and should be used to allocate resources.

2. Build momentum
Starting on day one of the combined firm, aim for early wins – new business brought in collaboratively, or new laterals attracted. Such wins are crucial psychologically, and momentum feeds on itself. Advertise the wins across the firm and explain their relation to the merger.

3. Develop and track but-for revenue
Develop a plan and a timeline to target new business neither firm would have sought or expected to win on its own. Then monitor any new business that came in where lawyers from both sides of the merger teamed up on the pitch. Whether this work really is but-for the merger will often be a judgement call, but over time a monitoring

"Be prepared to invest in travel to other offices, retreats and other formats for face-to-face meetings."

process should provide evidence for the benefits of combining. You can also use it to assess which approaches are working and which are not. Again, tout the successes.

4. Foster and measure cross-firm collaboration

Each major practice group and/or industry sector team should have a plan to integrate lawyers from both firms. Be prepared to invest in travel to other offices, retreats and other formats for face-to-face meetings. Once again, with measurement, the new firm will be able to assess what is working. For example, you will want to keep track of work that originated with lawyers from one legacy firm but is staffed by lawyers from the other, and from the office of one and the office of another. That is relatively easy to monitor and is a good barometer of collaboration and the degree to which you are achieving synergies. Again, announce examples that can serve as models.

5. Compensate partners for fulfilling the merger goals

The old business adage that you get the results you compensate people to achieve is no less true in law firms. If you want to make sure partners involve their counterparts from the other legacy firm on pitches or that they direct work to the most appropriate lawyers, regardless of which legacy firm they came from, reward it. If your compensation system does not give much weight to collaboration of this sort, now is the time to revisit it.

6. Leaders set the tone

As in any organisation, good law firm leaders set the tone, values and goals. In the case of a merger, those need to include a transparent, fair, generous, collaborative spirit and a dogged attention to the details of integration. If the merger was designed well during the negotiations, there should be enthusiasm and goodwill on both sides. But insecurities and suspicions can always crop up. Leaders of the legacy firms need to avoid doing anything that appears to favour their people. The contrary – that is, if they are seen to adopt ideas and champion the efforts of lawyers on the other side – will be a model down through the ranks.

Management perspectives

HUNTON ANDREWS KURTH

Almost from the outset, after Hunton & Williams and Andrews Kurth merged in 2018, partners subscribed to the notion that they were part of a unified firm. One sign of that was the extraordinary amount of cross-staffing that began within months of the merger. Collaboration among partners from the legacy firms also helped the new firm exploit new opportunities.

Wally Martinez, managing partner:

The biggest surprise was how quickly everyone saw themselves as being part of one law firm. That, frankly, really surprised me. I had prepared myself for some real social challenges over the first year, and the integration was incredible. Now, there were some fortuitous things. We [Hunton & Williams] traditionally had a very large partner meeting to ring out the old financial year and start the new one in April. The deal closed on April 2nd. A few weeks after that, everyone gathered in one place. The timing was lucky.

I guess you'd have to attribute the quick integration to the fact that the cultures, even though not completely the same – there were differences – were in many material respects very, very similar.

By the way, plan to spend, spend gleefully, a lot of money that first year on interoffice travel. Build that into your budget because you want to see that happen. You want to see people connecting.

We had different checkpoints to show how many matters existed where you had timekeepers from different legacy firms working together. By November, we were about 900 such matters. And this deal only went live on April 2nd.

It was important to be able to track that because, within the organization, it confirms the transaction. The only currency leaders of a law firm have – it's not titles or anything like that – it is their creditability. Whatever you say, you have to be able to show it. So it was important for us to have that tool because work on a merger doesn't stop once you close the deal, and it doesn't just stop when you've sorted out who is going to play what leadership role and things of that nature. It continues as you prove the case, which in turn leads to greater commitment broadly in the firm to ensure that the deal works.

In oil and gas, there are a lot of high-value transactions – restructurings, and so on – because companies need to do a deal to survive. We bring a broader skill set to those clients now. It's being led by the former Andrews Kurth M&A and restructuring folks in Houston, where we've been touching that industry forever, but now we can and do touch on more aspects of the business, using folks with deep experience in structured finance, for instance.

We've seen how the oil and gas capital markets lawyers in Houston, tax lawyers in Houston, and our existing REIT [real estate investment trust] tax lawyers in Richmond, Washington and New York became real thought leaders on the tools available to you as a REIT in the oil and gas space, and how they got together in presenting these opportunities to the investment banks.

Clearly, there are more opportunities to us combined, but you have to be proactive about it. So, we had transition teams in each practice group and within each industry focus area dedicated to identifying those opportunities that are truly complimentary and new. We put a lot of thought into it prior to the merger, but the real work happened post-merger as these folks got together and started working on identifying those opportunities.

SIDLEY & AUSTIN

If visible payoffs are not seen quickly, the success of the combination may be in question. But the process of realising synergies can re-energise the partnership.

Larry Barden, chair of management committee:

In any law firm merger, there will inevitably be some initial duplication of costs and personnel, which can put pressure on the immediate post-merger results. But the resulting higher costs can be absorbed – and actually support growth — assuming the merged firms can move quickly to capture the benefits of the merger on the revenue side.

The success of any merger will ultimately be measured by whether the merged firms can expand their respective client bases, grow revenues and profits, and enhance their reputations and market reach at a faster pace and magnitude together than the firms could have achieved individually. Simply having a larger profit pool to invest and support operations can be quite beneficial. Growth in revenues and profits post-merger can be expected to energize partners and open doors to not only recruiting new talent, but also motivating existing partners to tap their now expanded talent pool in pursuing new business.

If, on the other hand, the merged firm finds itself struggling to demonstrate to clients the benefits of the merger; if high partner attrition results, either from partners disenchanted with the merger or from increased poaching that often is triggered by mergers; if its initially higher cost structure precludes the merged firm from responding to growth opportunities; if management becomes too distracted with merger integration or struggles to create a shared vision for the firm; or the merger receives a poor market reaction, the merged firm could easily find itself off to a slow start, which could take several years to recover fully from.

Partner buy-in and support are critical to the success of law firm mergers. Partners who believe in the merger will think about "How can I make the most of this? How can I cross-sell better? Can I convince clients that we're competing on a different level pre-merger?"

Cultural fit is also critical and an essential responsibility of each firms' management. Because the number of partners participating in the merger diligence negotiations tends to be limited, most partners' confidence in the merger and trust in their new colleagues will develop in the initial post-merger interactions – those team meetings, those one-on-one conversations around the office, those opportunities to work together on firm committees or share in client pitches, the cross-firm staffing of projects. Partners need to come away from their initial interactions feeling impressed and comfortable with their new colleagues personally and professionally.

Notes

1 Tom Huddleston, Jr, "How a Move to Change Fueled Latham's Rise", *The American Lawyer*, 26 March 2012, available at https://amlawdaily.typepad.com/amlawdaily/2012/03/latham-chicago-expansion.html.
2 Based on the authors' analysis of data published in *The American Lawyer.*
3 Based on the authors' analysis of data published in *The American Lawyer.*
4 "Regional Law Firm Brand Indexes 2022: Clients seeking strong relationships from their outside law firms", Thompson Reuters, 23 March 2022, available at www.thomsonreuters.com/en-us/posts/legal/regional-law-firm-brand-indexes-2022/.
5 "Law Firms Sidley & Austin, Brown & Wood Back Merger", *The Wall Street Journal*, 24 April 2001, available at www.wsj.com/articles/SB988069728811839672.
6 Brenda Sapino Jeffreys, "Foley & Lardner to Merge With Dallas-Based Gardere", *Texas Lawyer*, 30 March 2018, available at www.law.com/texaslawyer/2018/03/30/foley-lardner-to-merge-with-dallas-based-gardere/.
7 Geert De Lombaerde, "Frost & Jacobs to merge with Louisville firm", *Cincinnati Business Courier*, 4 October 2000, available at www.bizjournals.com/cincinnati/stories/2000/10/02/daily26.html.
8 Brenda Sapino Jeffreys and Christine Simmons, "It's Official: Andrews Kurth and Hunton & Williams Will Merge", *Texas Lawyer*, 21 February 2018, available at www.law.com/texaslawyer/2018/02/21/its-official-andrews-kurth-and-hunton-williams-will-merge/.
9 Elie Mystal, "Hogan and Lovells Merger: All Systems Go", *Above the Law*, 15 December 2009, available at https://abovethelaw.com/2009/12/hogan-and-lovells-merger-all-systems-go/.
10 Jake Simpson, "Polsinelli Set To Acquire Novak Druce Attorneys", *Law360*, 16 February 2016, available at www.law360.com/articles/759653/exclusive-polsinelli-set-to-acquire-novak-druce-attorneys.

About the authors

Kent M Zimmermann
Principal, Zeughauser Group
zimmermann@consultzg.com

Kent M Zimmermann is one of the leading strategic advisers to law firm leaders in the United States, consulting on a number of the most high-profile firm mergers over the past decade. At any given time, he is typically advising on several active merger discussions.

Kent is also an ongoing strategic adviser to many category-leading firms, including five of the top 10 highest-grossing law firms in the world, helping them address the challenges and opportunities arising from the consolidation, specialisation, segmentation and globalisation of the legal services market. He believes that a well-informed and sophisticated understanding of the market and inside knowledge of the evolving strategies, cultures and best practices of high-performing law firms is essential to formulating plans to achieve a firm's full potential.

Kent serves as a Law.com fellow and contributes to *The American Lawyer*; his insights are regularly reported by Bloomberg Law, Law360 and Reuters.

Before joining Zeughauser Group, Kent was one of three equity partners who built a leading technology company, Hubbard One, which was acquired by Thomson Reuters in 2004. He lives in Newport Coast, California, with his family.

John E Morris
Managing editor, special projects, at a major global law firm
john.morris@nyc.rr.com

John E Morris earned a JD from Harvard Law School and practised law in California before becoming a legal, business and financial journalist. Over the course of a decade at *The American Lawyer*, where he served as the magazine's top editor and as editor-at-large, he wrote extensively about law firm mergers and the changing business of law in the United States and Europe. Later he was an editor at *The Deal*, Dow Jones and Bloomberg News.

John is the author of several previous books, including *King of Capital: The Remarkable Rise, Fall, and Rise Again of Steve Schwarzman and Blackstone* (2010), a history of the Blackstone Group and the private equity industry (co-authored with David Carey); *Subway: The Curiosities, Secrets, and Unofficial History of the New York City Transit System* (2020), an illustrated history of the New York subway system; and a history of the law firm Haynes and Boone, commissioned for its 50th anniversary in 2020. He is currently managing editor, special projects, at a major global law firm. He lives in New York City.

About Globe Law and Business

Globe Law and Business was established in 2005. From the very beginning, we set out to create law books which are sufficiently high level to be of real use to the experienced professional, yet still accessible and easy to navigate. Most of our authors are drawn from Magic Circle and other top commercial firms, both in the UK and internationally.

Our titles are carefully produced, with the utmost attention paid to editorial, design and production processes. We hope this results in high-quality publications that are easy to read, and a pleasure to own. Our titles are also available as ebooks, which are compatible with most desktop, laptop and tablet devices. In 2018 we expanded our portfolio to include journals and Special Reports, available both digitally and in hard copy format, and produced to the same high standards as our books.

In the spring of 2021, we were very pleased to announce the start of a new chapter for Globe Law and Business following the acquisition of law books under the imprint Ark Publishing. We are very much looking forward to working with our Ark authors, many of whom are well known to us, to further developing the law firm management list, and to welcoming our new Ark customers.

We'd very much like to hear from you with your thoughts and ideas for improving what we offer. Please do feel free to email me at sian@globelawandbusiness.com with your views.

Sian O'Neill
Managing director
Globe Law and Business
www.globelawandbusiness.com

www.ingramcontent.com/pod-product-compliance
Ingram Content Group UK Ltd.
Pitfield, Milton Keynes, MK11 3LW, UK
UKHW061902131026
9310IPUK00009B/88

9 781787 428454